Who is Tom McDonald? Why would you want to read his Southern short stories? Below you will find, a few of the reasons sent from readership about Tom McDonald's first publication, *When Memories Come Calling*.

Author Tom McDonald with catcher's mitt and his brother, John McDonald, holding the bat.

"Not only did I enjoy reading your life stories but many of my own came back 'a-calling. I do hope there is another writing on the way." Jerry Kelsoe

"This is one of the funniest books I have ever read. I can't wait for Tom's next book". Sheila Rhodes

"I have just finished reading your book and enjoyed it so much. There were so many things brought back to mind of that era. Weren't we fortunate to have lived in a more innocent time?" Sue Simmons

"You have taken me back to years long past...........gave me a chance to remember my father and mother and the hardships all families had. Thank you for sharing your life and book with me." Eddie Griffith

"Mr. McDonald did a fine job of making this reader laugh and cry while also taking me on a trip back to similar experiences and times. I loved every word." Berry Byington

To view *When Memories Come Calling* by Tom McDonald scan this link!

Dirt Road Memories

A Collection of Southern Short Stories

Tom McDonald

Published by:
Bluewater Publications

www.BluewaterPublications.com

Dedication

For our children, Amy and Will, who have brought us much joy.

Proverbs 23:24

The father of godly children has cause for joy. What a pleasure to have children who are wise.

Acknowledgment

The marvelous illustrations found in this book are the work of a true artist. Jackie Hastings, from Belmont, Mississippi, has generously allowed his drawings to grace the second of my books. His work brings much needed attention to my simple words as I attempt to tell a story. On the other hand, his drawings tell a story in a way which renders words totally unnecessary.

Contents

Introduction

As I mentioned in this same space of my first book, *When Memories Come Calling*, writing a book was never on my bucket list. Logically, if I never intended to write a first book, a second book would be equally unlikely. Hobnobbing with the literary crowd has not made me a blue blood and to mistake me for a legitimate author would be a bad mistake. However, I have been able to meet a lot of genuinely nice people and that is always a really good thing.

On a more serious note, after completing the first book, there seemed to be a lot more stories just waiting to be told. Besides, what else have I got to do? I offer a sincere word of thanks to those who went out of their way to tell me how much they enjoyed the *Memories* book. The prevailing sentiment seemed to me that stories in the book brought back memories of younger days or reminded them of similar predicaments in their own lives. Your words of encouragement are greatly appreciated.

The McClellan Saddle

Old Tony had a backbone that would have made a two by four look like a crosstie. At the time it didn't matter a bit. The night he half way fell out of the truck when the scoundrel we bought him from delivered him to the house, he could have had three legs and I would have still been as pleased as punch. In my estimation, the only difference between Tony and the Lone Ranger's horse, Silver, was color. You see, Tony was my very first horse. After years of dreaming and begging and delivering papers, I had finally saved up enough money to buy about one half of a real horse. This was after spending much of my young life galloping around the neighborhood on a cottonwood sapling with a stuffed sock for a head and only two short legs, mine.

For years, I was sort of a connoisseur of stick horses. The back alley behind our house was a veritable thicket of cottonwood saplings, which are ideal for stick horses. Anytime I felt the need to add a new horse to my herd, I simply took my hatchet and pocket knife and rounded up a few head. One could peel off some of the red outer bark to reveal the white inside and have a pinto pony in a flash. I kept a string of such horses for my own personal use corralled behind the house inside a fence also made of cottonwood saplings. On these stick horses I rounded up thousands of longhorns for the cattle drive to Montana, I rode with the Lone Ranger and Tonto to stand up for justice and give the bad guys a good licking. I won the Kentucky Derby numerous times and rescued dozens of damsels from villainous hands and galloped away into the sunset on my gallant steed. After a hard day of riding, I even went so far as to cool them down. It was common knowledge among all cowboys that a horse should never be ridden hard and put up wet. My fantasies ran wild but I knew it would be good training for the time I finally owned my own horse.

When that time finally arrived, we were living out in the country on a place owned by my oldest brother, Bill. There was plenty of pasture with a nice old barn and my daddy finally relented, if I would pay for it myself. It was my good luck that my brother, Johnny, still had his savings from the paper route we shared for several years and he agreed to pay half. In later years when my brain actually began to function, this generous gesture on his part puzzled me because he did not like horses, not even a little. Maybe he liked me more than I thought at the time or simply needed to invest his money. I might add here that later I contributed half the money for him to buy a short wave radio and I didn't particularly care for radios. He convinced me that we could become certified short wave operators and talk to people all over the world. It didn't take me long to lose interest because keeping up with all those dots and dashes was very confusing. It was difficult enough for me to talk with friends and family, much less some stranger halfway around the world.

Daddy knew a fellow who was a horse trader and told him to be on the lookout for a good kid's horse. In other words, he meant a horse that wouldn't run away if you set off a stick of dynamite and applied a cattle prod to his rear end at the same time. A kid's horse also allows kids to crawl over and under him without kicking or biting and will carry as many as can get on his back. A horse like this will return your love ounce for ounce and they are worth their weight in gold.

A lot of bad things have been said about horse traders over the years and every one of them applied in triplicate to the fellow who arrived at our house with my horse. He would cheat his grandmother out of her false teeth if he could make a dollar. It occurred to me years later that the rascal had good reason to deliver Tony after dark. The old horse appeared drastically different during the light of the day. He was well along in years and looked a lot like the old horse Ichabod Crane rode when being chased by the Headless Horseman in the *Legend of Sleepy Hollow,* if you know what I mean. He was a big bay, not big in weight but in height. Be that as it may, he was still my horse and I loved him dearly, at first sight. The two to three hours between the phone call that a horse was in a truck headed for our house and the time he arrived were probably the two to three happiest hours of unadulterated joy in my entire life.

Many years later I made the mistake of buying another horse from this very fellow, who had someway managed to escape the gallows. When we went to his place to look at her, a nice strawberry roan mare, several of his lackeys had to chase her across the pasture and rope her just to get her to the barn. This was not a good sign. A good lesson learned was to never purchase a horse from an owner who describes it as "spirited." That probably means the horse really belongs in the saddle bronc competition at a rodeo. Somewhere along the line, the mare had never learned the meaning of "whoa." Her mouth was as hard as a locust post. During the time we owned her, she broke the arm of two different people by running away and crashing into a tree or fence after refusing to stop. Unfortunately, one of them was my brother, Johnny. From then on, he had good reason to dislike horses. She also had the disagreeable habit of trying to kick anyone with the nerve to attempt to get in the saddle. With one foot in the stirrup, one had to be especially cagey and nimble in order to avoid a vicious sideswipe with her rear leg. If she failed to nail you with the kick, her next move was to bolt away at full speed while the rider was half-way in the saddle. Other than a few flaws, she was a nice horse.

4

One good lesson I did learn from the horse we called Lightning was that one can overcome fear and not let it control something you really want to do. Like facing up to a bully, one day I finally decided I would ride her and I did; that day and many more days in the years to come. And, like all bullies, she wasn't as tough as she thought and eventually settled down to become a pretty decent horse, if you liked to ride real fast.

Tony's height and my lack of it presented a problem right off the bat. Normally, the stirrups of a saddle could have been adjusted to fit my short stature. The problem was I did not have a saddle. I had an old bridle that fit around one ear and behind the other with a straight bit and reins made from bailing twine. I could easily have done without a bridle because Tony was not one to act impulsively. A stump came in handy for mounting purposes but they weren't always available. My few attempts to emulate the Roy Rogers method of mounting by making a run from behind the horse and vaulting onto his back were a dismal failure. Short legs and a tall horse tend to discourage this type of show-boating. Learning to ride bareback was my only option. It took a lot of tumbles and a lot of stumps but perseverance does pay off and in a lot of ways other than learning to mount and ride a horse.

Daddy was aware of my problem but did not offer to buy a saddle. So, I learned to ride without a saddle and was glad I did. It's sort of like learning to drive a straight shift car rather than one with an automatic transmission. If you can drive a straight shift, everything else is a piece of cake. If everyone had to take their driver's license road test in a vehicle with a straight shift, a lot of very dangerous people would be kept off the road, thus making the world a safer place. The same with a horse; if you can ride a horse at a dead run bareback, the luxury of a saddle is like sitting in a recliner. However, there are drawbacks to riding a skinny horse without a saddle, especially one with a backbone like Tony's. This was about the time in my life when my voice started to change. In hindsight, it seemed my voice stayed in the high pitched range a lot longer than my friends who did not own a horse. Maybe it was due to the onset of puberty or it could have been the result of the sharp backbone without a saddle.

One day Daddy came home from work and said he knew a fellow who had a saddle to sell for ten dollars. It so happened I didn't have ten dollars but Daddy had a solution. He had a pile of old lumber and bricks he wanted to use but couldn't use them in their present condition. The way he figured it, it would be worth about ten dollars if someone would pull the nails out of the lumber and then stack it neatly inside the barn. Then, clean all the mortar off the bricks with a hammer and chisel. Meanwhile, he would tell the fellow to hold the saddle until I could earn the ten bucks. A ten dollar loan was apparently

5

out of the question. It must have been because of a serious lack of collateral by the recipient of the loan. Working after school and on Saturdays, I polished off that task in a few weeks.

Finally, the day arrived when we were going to collect my very first real saddle. I had already imagined something with a lot of leather straps and silver buckles; sort of like you would see in a parade. I slowly counted out the ten, crumpled one-dollar bills into his hand and the old fellow returned with a saddle unlike any I had ever seen. It was a McClellan Saddle. These saddles were used by the United States Cavalry when horse soldiers were chasing Geronimo across the plains of Texas. They were designed by and named for General George B. McClellan, at one time the commander of the Union Army during the Civil War and later a presidential candidate. The old saddle had no horn to speak of and was open in the middle. This feature was to reduce weight and allow air flow to the backs of the cavalry horses after many long hours under saddle. There were no decorated leather skirts and the stirrup was a wooden hoop held by a single strap of leather. The fact that I had just bought one was ample proof that they were designed for the long haul to withstand the rigors of military use in the field. Though not exactly what I had in mind, it was better than no saddle at all. While I generally rode alone, the saddle was a good conversation piece when I encountered another rider. The question, "What is that?" was heard quite often.

Tony and the saddle eventually became the property of one of my nieces who loved the old horse as much, if not more, than I did. I was pleasantly surprised only a few years ago, while visiting my niece, to find the saddle was still in her possession, although not in a usable condition.

It was good that I had to spend my money to buy my own horse and saddle. It seems to me that today a lot of young folks expect their first job to be that of company president, their first car to be a Mercedes and their first house to be a mansion. Starting at the bottom and working one's way up is not a popular policy with a lot of folks. In my opinion, it would be good for them to spend some time riding stick horses. Old Tony was not a thoroughbred or parade horse and my first saddle would have been an embarrassment to some folks, but not to me.

During my life I have been privileged to own many horses, some registered with papers, but not one of them meant as much to me as Tony. Just thinking of the miles I traveled on that horse sitting on that old saddle still brings a smile to my face today. Together we rode dusty back roads, galloped across unfenced fields and splashed across creeks. Occasionally caught out in the rain, I would dismount and hunker beneath him for shelter. Sometimes he was an old cow pony and other times he was Man-Of-War, but he was my friend and companion all the time. It was not unusual to leave home early and return late. Tony could be trusted not to wander off so I could easily get off and lay in the grass, sip the nectar from honey suckle blooms and watch the clouds change shape while he happily grabbed a free meal in a nearby patch of clover. A lot of good things can be said about being a boy with a horse in the 1950's.

The author pictured holding the old McClellan saddle he purchased for the pricey sum of ten dollars as a boy.

Jackie Hastings

A Tale of Two Mules

The epicenter of muledom has to be Columbia, Tennessee, in early spring of each year. It is here in this small town in the south central part of the state that thousands flock every year to pay tribute to a critter that has been considered a low and humble servant of man for centuries. Anyone who may have mistakenly thought the lowly mule had been turned out to pasture, so to speak, can see this creature in all its glory during this time. The event is modestly known as Mule Day but that is a gross understatement of what really goes on. They kick off on Monday and don't conclude until the following Sunday and this constitutes more than a day on my calendar. Mules of every size, color, heritage and religious preference can be viewed in such numbers that one might conclude mules have suddenly taken over the world. Mule lovers come out of the woodwork to watch show mules, work mules, riding mules, trick mules, racing mules, roping mules, jumping mules and mules who do absolutely nothing worthwhile show off their stuff. Those who have no stuff to show off just stand around and wait to be fed, which is sort of typical of the reputation of all the mules I have been around.

As I recall, the mules of my day were not known for their color, size or for any unusual talent they might possess. They were not normally lauded, bathed, manicured and groomed like beauty contestants. Any self-respecting mule would have been embarrassed by all the attention. Mules were considered to be strictly work animals and lived a pretty rough life in a lot of cases. Many worked from sunup to sundown for little or no compensation. If they were talked about at all it was for their stubborn disposition. Honestly, this bad reputation may have been a direct result for having to do so much work. It could also stem from the fact that a mule is a cross between a horse mare and a jack. For all the world to know that your father was a jackass would create a host of personality problems. Mules may have gotten a bad rap because of the antics of a few bad apples and it has taken generations to set the record straight. I believe this is what is actually going on in Columbia, Tennessee, and they are succeeding mightily.

While we are setting the record straight, I must admit that the information I may have on mules does not come from actually owning one of the critters. The truth is, I have never owned a mule but I have owned several donkeys, which are sort of a mule's first cousin but the donkeys won't admit this kinship publicly. At any rate, growing up in the South when I did, I was around a lot of mules and have heard stories about mules all my life.

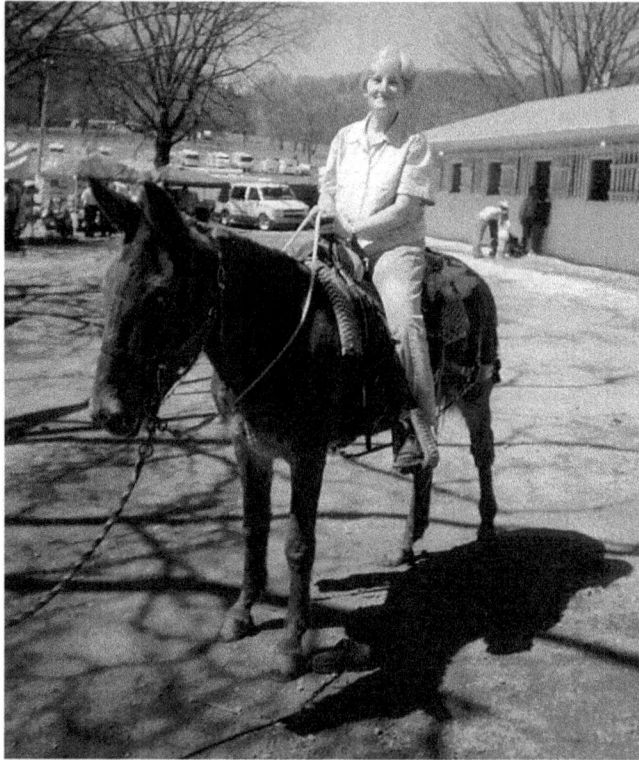

The author's wife, Margo, ready to ride a sorrel
mule at Mule Day in Columbia, Tennessee.

For those of us who grew up in the vicinity of a general store, we know for a fact they were a great source of information, and often misinformation, about a myriad of subjects. Fortunately, there were several such stores in the community where I lived and there was one in particular which seemed to be frequented by some old men who claimed to know a lot about every conceivable subject, including mules. One of the merchants, after a lengthy discourse on a topic of interest, would always conclude his remarks with the statement, "And boys, them ar's facts." That statement in itself was very debatable because, for the most part, a fact was whatever they wanted it to be at the time. It is quite possible they didn't know as much as they claimed because their reputation for telling the truth was suspect. The old geezers had been caught telling bald-face lies more than once and, like mules, had a hard time setting the record straight. There was a rumor that one of the churches in the community actually considered diverting a missionary from assignment in Africa to working in the general stores as a full time missionary. The fields were certainly ripe to harvest. Apparently they had nothing else to do other than sit

10

around on the bench outside the store in warm weather and spin yarns, many of which involved mules they were acquainted with as boys on the farm. Cold weather did not damper their cock-and-bull fabrications but only forced them inside where stories of equal caliber were told while sitting on the bench around the wood heater. Most of the giant box stores of today would probably not want them around because I have always suspected they were bad for business. Unfortunately, they knew each other's stories by heart because of sheer repetition over the years and always took great delight when someone of my ilk happened by and provided some fresh ears, so to speak. My daddy had taught me to be courteous to my elders so I was the recipient of many of their tales, although sometimes reluctantly, especially if I was in a hurry. It was never a good idea to let them know you were headed to see a girl and didn't have the time to sit for a spell. This little gem of information always caused the conversation to take a drastic turn, generally for the worse, and drift to topics which they seemed to remember with a great deal of fondness from their younger days. However, they did claim to know a lot about mules and were more than willing to share this information.

As a boy growing up in East Florence, not every resident had a vehicle and there were several families who earned their living with mules by breaking up garden plots, hauling a wagon load of firewood and various other mule-worthy chores. They also used them as a means of transportation around the community. It was not unusual to see an entire family riding in an old wagon pulled by a team of mules. The same sort of economy can be seen today by visiting the Amish community a few miles north of Lawrenceburg, Tennessee. The work provided by mules and horses is as vital to their existence today as it was during the early settlement of this nation.

This brings to mind a story about my brother, Bobby. Despite being repeatedly warned by our daddy not to hang around and be seen with a certain disreputable fellow who always owned and traded mules, our brother could not resist the temptation. Actually, most of our daddy's sons could resist everything except temptation. This seemed to be a family trait. The fellow in question was coarse and profane according to our mother. She also believed him to be under the influence of demon rum on those days he would hitch up his team of mules and drive like a bat out of hades back and forth through the streets of the community. The boys in the area thought him to be something like a Roman charioteer during these mad dashes and we enjoyed them immensely. Come to think of it, there seemed to be a lot about the old fellow my mother didn't like but it is not unusual at all for mothers and their sons to admire vastly different traits in other people. I suppose this was the chief reason the boys of the neighborhood were attracted to him like bees to honey. There was a good possibility she had influenced Daddy in a negative manner toward the colorful old character and he felt an obligation to warn us to stay away from his place. The truth of the matter is that all mule traders have a bad reputation because that seems to be the nature of their chosen profession. Show me a mule or horse trader with a good reputation and I will claim to have seen a miracle. The old fellow in question was no different in that respect.

There was always something interesting going on around his old barn and most of the boys in the community frequently felt the need to drop by to check out the situation. One day we were traveling up Sweetwater Avenue and I was in the back seat of Daddy's old car with my brother, Johnny. As Daddy pulled out to pass a wagon being pulled by a pair of mules, we looked up and saw our brother, Bobby, proudly sitting on the seat right beside the old man Daddy had warned us about. Before we arrived on the scene with Daddy, our brother was acting sort of like the Grand Marshall of a big parade. He was laughing and waving at people along the street like he was some sort of a celebrity. However, his mood changed in the blink of an eye. Bobby's reaction when he saw our daddy's car alongside the wagon was very comical. Displaying the reflexes of a cat, he did sort of a back flip off the seat into the wagon bed in an attempt to avoid being seen. We were as silent as a church mouse in the back seat because we could see our daddy's neck turn red and now was not the time for flippant conversation. The red neck was ample evidence our brother had been spotted and would be in for a trip to the cellar when he arrived back at the house. Daddy was not one to make idle threats and Bobby took what was coming to him like a man. The fact of the matter was he had no choice and knew our daddy was not running a debate club. He had been caught red-handed and a glib tongue would only make matters worse. However, research and experience have proven corporal punishment is not always one hundred percent effective. A few days later I found myself sneaking around the back alley behind the old man's mule barn. We often traveled via back alleys because we didn't want to be spotted out front of certain establishments. It just so happened, I spotted my brother Bobby in the barn helping the old fellow tighten a loose shoe on one of his mules. Even at my young age I found it was possible for the fear of self-incrimination to overpower a loose tongue. It was always a good idea to be able to call in favors from older brothers somewhere down the road. In such a case, silence was indeed golden.

Mules have continued to be a fixture on many of the farms in the rural South in spite of the availability of machines which do a lot more work in an hour than a team of mules could ever accomplish in a whole day. A friend of mine I worked with for a long time frequently told the story of growing up working his daddy's mules on a few acres of ground where his family skimped out a meager living in extremely rural Fayette County. During his high school years, he continued to work with mules all the while trying to convince his daddy to trade the mules for a tractor. It was always his contention had his daddy done so, he would never have left the farm and eventually gone on to college. He later became a dominant figure in Alabama politics and came within a few percentage points of being elected governor of our state. This turn of events never would have happened had his daddy not loved his mules so much. He absolutely refused to part with them for a new-fangled invention which he believed couldn't possibly last very long and would never take the place of mules in the field. This same pattern of migration caused many children of the South to give up working the fields with mules and hoes to seek a less demanding life style.

While in college, I worked for a while for the Department of Agriculture in what was called the Agricultural Stabilization and Conservation section. My job was to go around to the farms growing cotton and measure the amount of acreage they had planted. I did this by using a long measuring chain and then plotting the dimensions of the field onto a large aerial photograph. This was then measured on some sort of machine back in the office and the exact acreage determined. For years the government had been in the business of stabilizing the price of cotton by limiting the amount grown. Each farmer applied for an allotment and could only plant the amount allotted for that year. If my measuring determined he had over planted, then he was forced to plow up the acreage in excess of his allotment. Therefore, when a cotton scout showed up, the farmer felt like he had to give us his complete attention to make sure we didn't screw up his allotment.

The area known as the bend of the river in southwestern Lauderdale County is flat and fertile and the fields frequently measure in the hundreds of acres. On the other hand, in the northwestern part of the county the land is hilly and flat land is at a premium. The available flat land suitable for cotton is found in the numerous creek bottoms which are surrounded by heavily forested hills. The area is more suited for pulp wood and timber than for cotton. The few cotton fields in the area are small and found in the hollows between hills. Therefore, it was much easier to walk from one hidden hollow to the next instead of trying to drive, which was often not possible anyway considering the fact there were no roads and a lot of springs and creeks flowing through the low ground.

So it was that on this fine day during the summer of 1966, I was strolling between a series of very small patches of cotton in extreme, northwest Lauderdale County. The day was going to be a bust for me money-wise because cotton scouts were paid based on the number of acres we surveyed. It would take most of a day to get to all these fields, survey and plot them on the map then return to my truck. There were a total of four to five fields but no more than twenty acres of cotton altogether. If the same amount of time had been spent in the bend of the river area I would have been in big money because the fields there were huge and had well-defined boundaries. A truck could also be driven around the perimeter of each field which cut out on a lot of walking. Some of these patches had recently been in trees and bull-dozed out only after the timber had been cut making them extremely difficult to plot on my aerial photos. Piles of stumps were still evident around the edges and made ideal hiding places for rattlesnakes and copperheads. Since I worked around the edges of a field, I had to be very careful.

While we were being trained to do our jobs, we were warned by an old pro to be very careful and not to be poking around in places where we had no business, especially when we were in isolated areas. I had discovered this to be true several weeks earlier when I happened to stumble across an illegal moonshine still while searching for a cotton field in very similar circumstances. This part of the county had long been a haven for moonshiners because it was very isolated and there were countless streams running out of the hills and down the hollows: both essential elements for the production of illegal liquor. We were told repeatedly if we happened upon a still we were to keep walking, not to stop and look around and not to appear interested in the surroundings. It was almost a certainty the operators were somewhere close-by watching and some of them were really bad people. In my situation, I had smelled the sour mash and was about to turn around when I realized I had already walked past the still. My only option was to keep walking and I did, never looking back. On my return trip I walked out to the dirt road and an extra couple of miles back to my parked truck so that I could keep well clear of the still. It is never a good idea to kick a sleeping dog.

Encountering another still under the circumstances would have been much less surprising than what I was about to experience. From a logging road to my right I was mildly startled to see a mule coming toward me at an angle. This was a rather large mule and one that was sort of blue in color. Its coat was white but had enough hair of another color that it gave the animal the appearance of being blue, or at least it did to me. The mule was fully harnessed and happened to be pulling a large poplar log behind it. Even more astonishing, it was all by itself. The path the mule was on intersected the woods road I was on and the critter walked right past me without even acknowledging my presence. Some folks might consider it an insult to be ignored by a mule but, other than stopping for a chat, I don't know what else the mule could have done. The critter seemed to have a destination in mind and I was not about to interfere with the mule's affairs. Besides, in my youth I had been told by a man at a general store who knew mules that some mules would work for a man twenty years just for the opportunity to kick him one time. What did I know? This could be one of the very mules he had in mind and if it was going to kick somebody it wouldn't be me. Based on what I knew of the situation, a brute the size of this mule always had the right of way.

This was indeed a strange occurrence but I heeded my training to mind my own business and continued on my way toward the next field. The distance between us slowly increased and soon the log- dragging mule was completely out of sight as the road snaked its way through the woods and across several streams. As I walked along, I pondered over what was probably going on. I had heard of mules trained to the point where they worked basically without constant human supervision. Apparently, this mule was travelling back and forth between the logging site, which was probably far up in the hills, and the logger's truck. I suspected the truck was parked somewhere ahead of me close to the road. The man cutting the trees would hook each log to the mule and the mule would drag the log to the truck where another person would unhook the log from the mule and allow the mule to return to go back for another log. The appearance of the ground in front of me indicated this was not the first trip for the mule. This system saved somebody a heap of walking. In a few minutes I was to learn my summation of the plan in progress was right on the money.

I arrived at a split in the trail where it was obvious the mule had veered to the left. The small patch of cotton was visible to the right and I headed in that direction so I could finish my work and get out of the woods as soon as possible. Maybe my next batch of work would be more profitable. As I measured and plotted the small cotton field, I could hear the sound of the logging truck only a short distance away. Those old trucks loaded logs onto the bed by using machine power instead of man power and made a heap of noise. Two arms sat on the ground attached to the truck and alongside the bed. The log was positioned onto the arms and a lever was pulled, releasing the hydraulic power generated by a pump on the truck. This caused the two arms to move rather violently from lying flat on the ground into an upright position, thus tossing the log through the air onto the bed of the truck. It was possible for the pile of logs on the truck to reach a good height from the ground, far higher than mere man power could ever achieve.

My work was done and I was headed out for the long walk back to my truck when I heard a sound which I hope to never hear again. It can only be described as a blend of animal and human screams which could not possibly reach such a level except in a moment of sheer terror. There was the distinct sound of a mule braying but at an extremely high pitch with a clearly audible dose of panic. A voice which was unmistakably human was also a part of the mix but at a much lower volume. It was obvious something terrible had happened to the poor mule. As impossible as it seemed, the noise grew louder as I began running toward the sound. Bursting from the woods, I came across a sight that was hard to comprehend and get my brain around. It was such a seldom seen sight I would venture to say only a few people in the history of the world had ever witnessed what was before my eyes. The truck was parked in a small clearing and was about half-loaded with mostly poplar logs. That was not the unusual part. However, astraddle the top log on the truck was the blue mule, still terror-stricken and braying for all it was worth. Running around the truck and all the while looking up at the mule was a young man of about my age. He saw me about the same time I saw him and came out to meet me before I could reach the truck. Obviously, the first question to come out of my mouth was, "What in the world has happened here?" His response was short but straight to the point, "I done loaded Bugger's mule."

At this point it seems necessary to do some "splaining," as some folks might put it. The logging rig, including the mule, was apparently the property of one Lonzie "Bugger" Smith. The aforementioned Mr. Smith, or Bugger as we will refer to him from this point forward, was a resident widely known by locals and probably law enforcement. Logging timber and pulp wood provided the visible and taxable portion of Bugger's income. However, it was widely rumored that the lion's share of his money came from producing the illegal whiskey for which this particular part of the county was widely known. In other words, he was a moonshiner. This is the type of information one can easily pick up by hanging around old men in general stores. Maybe I should temper my words somewhat and say he was only an alleged moonshiner at the time. It was public knowledge that many years ago he had been convicted and served time for being a real moonshiner but now, since he had not been arrested, charged and convicted again, it was only alleged that he had returned to his old trade. Since his release from the lockup, Bugger had supposedly changed his ways and was following the straight and narrow. His reformed face consisted of the logging business which seemed to be on the horns of a dilemma at the moment.

Bugger had a two man and a mule logging crew. In addition to the young man standing by the truck and the blue mule sitting atop a pile of logs on the truck, there had to be another crew member. Apparently, that was the fellow at the other end of the path being followed by the mule. Someone had to be out in the woods doing the actual felling of the trees and chaining the logs in order for the mule to bring them back to the truck.

Logging is a very difficult way to make a living, even during the best of times. During the summer the logger contends with stifling hot weather with any chance of a cooling breeze muffled by the surrounding trees. His workplace is a home for snakes, ticks, yellow jackets and hornets, not to mention falling trees and limbs which are unpredictable and have killed many a logger. If this weren't enough, he works with a saw in his hand which is capable of removing any part of the body within a split second. During the winter the logger has a reprieve from the biting critters but still has to dodge the limbs and trees. Bitter cold and mud are a way of life. This is a profession in which the man at the low end of the totem pole, in the woods or at the truck, has absolutely no chance of advancement or to move up the pay scale. It is a dangerous and unpredictable job and, by comparison, moonshining may seem a better choice. There is one thing for certain and that is the money is a whole lot better.

After calming down, the young fellow explained how the mule had managed to find its way atop the log pile. It is hard for loggers to find and keep good help because of the reasons mentioned above. Also, some of the helpers are often tempted to drink up yesterday's meager pay and miss the next few days in a drunken stupor. Bugger had hired the fellow at the truck out of desperation to help get some logs out of the woods and put some money in his pocket. He would undoubtedly have preferred a more experienced hand but he had no other option at the time. The job description was quite simple. The mule drags the log up to the side of the truck. Next, the log is positioned directly over the two loading arms. The mule is unhitched from the log and moved safely away from the loading arms, which are quite dangerous. A lever protruding from the side of the truck is then pulled, releasing the arms and the log is tossed onto the truck. The arms return to their original position on the ground to await the next log. It was at this point the issue became quite muddied. Somehow, after the last log had been loaded, the arms were prepared for the next log and the mule was turned around to go back to the woods. Apparently, the mule passed too close to the truck and inadvertently triggered the lever. In addition to being stubborn, mules can be like children in another way by not paying attention to important details. Unfortunately, this occurred while the mule was directly above the arm and consequently, caught the mule in the stomach area and tossed him aboard the truck. The mule was fortunate not to be killed, or severely injured in the process. However, all the thrashing around atop the rough logs had scuffed him up somewhat but it seemed to be okay. Of course, that could not be determined until the mule was somehow unloaded.

It was as this point I decided to take my leave. The tree cutter in the woods was not Bugger but another hired hand. Somehow, Bugger would have to be fetched to the scene and figure out what to do. He was the brain trust of the organization and would have to make all the decisions. A decision of this magnitude was far above the pay scale of the on-site hired help. Obviously, they would have to have some sort of a machine to lift the mule because it was situated about eight feet off the ground. A mule of this type was far too valuable to risk breaking a leg by simply dragging him off the logs back to the ground. As a matter of fact, in terms of money, the mule was worth far more to Bugger than his hired help or the truck. This process could take hours and I had places to go and cotton to measure just to pay for the day's gas. My fervent hope has always been that the mule escaped his ordeal to log another day. If the mule did survive the incident unscathed, I imagine he would stay clear of logging trucks for a long time. They are not always the dumb brutes they are made out to be. My escape from the scene was painless and I carried with me a memory to last a life time. Not everyone gets to see a blue mule sitting atop a log truck in the middle of nowhere. A fellow could live a long, long time and never have the opportunity to witness such an event.

Amazingly enough, my next major encounter with a mule took place only a short time after the incredible mule loading incident. My cotton checking assignments could be anywhere from the Tennessee state line to the north, the Tennessee River to the south and the Mississippi state line to the west. This was a heap of territory and included a lot of working mules during the 1960's. At that time it was still very commonplace for many landowners in the South to use sharecroppers to maximize the use of their property. There was no practical way they would be able to hire enough help to do all that had to be done. Under this age-old system, families were allowed to live on the property and work for them in exchange for a place to live. In place of a salary they were given a share of the crops produced. The life of a share cropper was as difficult as that of a logger, and maybe more so. Much of the work force in factories of the North was comprised of these folks seeking a better way of life. As a rule, all the landowners were white men and the sharecroppers could be either white or black. I came across many of both races while measuring the cotton on property owned generally by whites.

It was on just such a farm between the Oakland and Rhodesville communities in the western part of the county I found myself, again during the summer of 1966. I had completed my measuring job and had gotten the landowner's signature on the paperwork when the next mule saga began and lasted only a few short minutes.

As we were concluding our business, a young African-American boy of about twelve came running from across the field shouting, "Mista B, Mista B. you gotta come quick." By the time he arrived where we were standing, he was practically out of breath. The owner of the place said, "What is it Charley, what happened?" In some circles, Charley's response would have made no sense. He said, "You know that ole red mule, he done balked." Mr. B. knew exactly what Charley was talking about because he had dealt with mules all his life. In fact, he had made a good deal of money buying green unbroken mules at the end of the summer and breaking them to work during the winter. When planting time came along in the spring, he always had several well-trained mules to sell. They could work alone or in tandem with another mule. Thus, they were highly sought after by farmers both near and far and had provided an excellent source of income. The conversation continued. Mr. B. wanted to know where the mule was at the time. Charley calmly told him the mule was lying on its back in the bottom of the ditch at the foot of the hill. It seems some of Mr. B.'s tenants were using the mule to pull stumps and it just decided to work no longer. When a mule makes this decision, it is pretty much a final one unless someone knows what to do. No amount of pulling, shoving or whipping will move a balking mule until it decides on its own to move. The worst part about it is that if a balking mule is allowed to get away with it, it will not be worth anything because it could not be counted on in the future to do any work. It could be compared to a child throwing a tantrum in a toy store. If it works, why stop doing it? Mr. B. instructed the boy to go back and tell them not to do anything else to the mule and he would be there in a minute. By this time my interest had risen more than a few notches. Since I was on my way out, I asked if I could go along and watch and it was okay with the mule guy.

Following along in my truck, we soon reached the site of the balking mule. A crowd of men, all African-American, were standing around a shallow ditch and, sure enough, right smack in the bottom was a reddish colored mule on its back with all four legs pointed straight up in the air. Mr. B. calmly got out of his truck and walked toward the ditch with the crowd of men parting before him. Surveying the situation he told Charley to get the empty dog food can lying on the ground and go to the truck and fill it with water. In his haste to return with the water, he spilled about half of it but Mr. B. told him it was enough. The farmer made his way down into the ditch and stood at the mule's head holding the half-full can of water in one hand. I could easily tell he was a man who knew exactly what he was doing and this was not his first encounter with a balking mule.

Quick as a cat, he dropped down on his rear behind the head of the mule while wrapping both legs around its neck and locking them under the chin in one quick motion. Before the mule could react, he had grabbed it under the chin, lifted its nose toward the sky and poured the contents of the can into the mule's nostrils. He then clamped both hands around the mouth and nose cutting off any air and held the head in a vice-like grip. The mule thrashed, kicked and tried to breathe but to no avail. A mule or horse cannot get to its feet with its head pinned so the mule was basically helpless. No doubt the mule was convinced it was dying and would have given most anything in the world for the opportunity to get up and pull some more stumps out of the ground. Mules, as well as people, often suffer from making bad decisions. Anyone within reach of its flailing hooves would have been severely injured but the only person in the ditch was the man holding the head and he was totally out of reach. I was truly watching a professional at work. I suppose in an operation like this timing is everything. At apparently just the right time, the man released his grip on the mule's head and scrambled out of the ditch before the mule knew he was gone. Suddenly, a volcano of water, snot and particles of hay spewed forth from the mule's nose and shot at least ten feet into the air. The mule struggled to its feet and stood legs askew, while its lungs continued to gasp for more air. The drama having passed, the old farmer calmly told the assembled crowd to hitch the mule back and make him work the rest of the day. As meek as a kitten by this time, the mule was led out of the ditch and gladly resumed the task at hand, having learned his lesson the hard way. Little did I know at the time, but I had just been an eye witness to the water-boarding of a mule. Anything that would work on a balking mule would surely make a terrorist sing long and loud.

It seems to me that there are many of the human species who have a longing for fame, no matter how fleeting. The Guinness Book of World Records is ample evidence many of us look for immortality, or our fifteen minutes of fame as some would say. Probably more than one mule has been loaded onto a log truck during the course of human history. Mules working in the immediate vicinity of a log truck on a daily basis would increase the odds of this happening, even if it doesn't occur often. I know for a fact that more than one balking mule has been through the water boarding ordeal because the man in charge knew exactly what he was doing. The question is how many people have witnessed these two extremely rare events within a few weeks of each other? I venture to say, not many! Surely, my fifteen minutes of fame would involve more than a couple of mules during the summer of 1966.

Exercise Follies

Like most other members of the human race, I am prone to look for scapegoats when events in my life take a turn for the worse. Why should I accept the blame when it is much easier to blame someone else? Politicians did not invent this human trait but I believe they have pretty much honed it to perfection. A politician who accepts blame is about as rare as a Methodist who doesn't like casseroles. While I would love to point an accusing finger at politicians for my current dilemma, I cannot in good conscience lay the blame at their feet. Instead, there is no doubt coaches are at fault.

During a life which apparently took place eons ago, I made the mistake of becoming interested in sports. Not satisfied with simply being a spectator, I showed up for try-outs for a variety of sports and on rare occasions, actually became a part of a few teams. This was generally a matter of crunching numbers. It takes a certain number of players to conduct a legitimate practice so coaches were frequently forced to lower the bar considerably in order to get down to my level of expertise. My current problems are simply an extension of many coaches' obsession that the team members engage in strenuous physical exercise in order to "get into shape," as they would say. The use of that particular phrase has been responsible for more misery over the years than most of us can stand. We have spent millions on equipment, really neat exercise apparel, doctors' visits and prescription pain medication which could have been re-directed at erasing the national debt with a healthy surplus to boot. But no, we wasted it all on ourselves!

Unfortunately, when I became an adult, my doctor also managed to become fixated on the subject of my physical well-being. His incessant nagging became about as bad as that of a coach except there was not a lot of shouting involved. Instead, he did make some very dire predictions about not living a long time if I didn't change my ways. Due to the fact that my doctor saw me much less often than my coach, it was much easier to break my frequent promises to do better. However, at very rare intervals, I have seen the wisdom of my doctor's advice and vowed to actually do something about it. My height to weight index had become terribly skewed over the years since high school. It seemed I was either too short for my weight, or too heavy for my height. My condition placed me in the predicament of being too heavy for light activity and too light for heavy activity. Whatever, something had to be done.

The phrase, "keeping fit," is now preached on every television show encompassing thousands of channels and is the subject of the lead article of every glossy magazine cover in the Wal-Mart check-out line. Exercises to keep fit, diets to keep fit, foods not to eat to keep fit, toothpaste and tooth brushes to keep fit, mattresses to buy to keep fit, the proper shoes and clothes to help us keep fit are screaming out at us at every turn. We can't escape! This might be the right time to put the hay right down where the goats can get at it. The fact of the matter is that my body has grown quite content with itself. My muscles tell me constantly they are not interested in being toned. The flab I have accumulated over the years prefers to stay right where it is and not die a horrible death at the hands of some barbaric exercise routine devised by sadists. Why we are not able to let well-enough alone is beyond my comprehension!

So, somewhere early in our married life, Margo and I reluctantly bought into this, "business about fitness," rubbish and thus began a sorry history of making poor decisions about how best to accomplish this task. Since both of us had jobs and there were two children in the house, it was not feasible to leave town and spend a few weeks at a trendy weight-loss spa which both of us would have preferred. It was even difficult for us to take much needed walks down our driveway on a consistent basis. We had long given up on the medical profession developing a little fitness pill which would eliminate all the stress and hard work associated with actually having to exercise. Obviously, we needed an in-home machine of some kind which would tone our bodies and make us happy. We noticed right off that the people using exercise machines on television were always smiling and seemed to be having a jolly good time. This was in sharp contrast to the poor, unsmiling souls we witnessed jogging along the roads. We soon concluded anyone who can grin like a mule that is eating saw briars while engaged in strenuous physical activity is obviously demented and cannot be trusted to tell the truth about anything, much less a machine capable of inflicting severe pain.

If my memory serves me correctly, our decision was made for our first purchase while watching a winter Olympic event called cross-country skiing. The commentators spent considerable time touting all the marvelous benefits of that sport. Well, living in the Deep South, cross-country skiing was not something with which we were real familiar. Miraculously, in just a very few minutes, a commercial was aired featuring a machine called the Nordic Track Cross Country ski machine. What a coincidence! Owners of this remarkable machine could enjoy all the cardio benefits of cross country skiing without the inconvenience of going outside in cold weather and suffering hypothermia. In addition, it could be tucked away in a corner of the house and we could become fit in the privacy of our own home without the scrutiny of the self-righteous eyes of those tanned, sleek, skinny people who frequent gyms and health clubs.

In spite of the fact that the machine cost us several weeks' salary and most of our children's college fund, we took the plunge and waited eagerly for its arrival. As parents of two children, Margo and I had learned to be wary of the phrase, "some assembly may be required," in conjunction with Christmas. For some reason, Santa's elves did not have the time to actually assemble the toys he left at our house for our children and seemed to think we could handle it on our own. It is for this very reason I have come to believe that Santa is actually anti-family and is responsible for perpetrating a gigantic hoax on most of the world. If a marriage can survive an all-nighter on Christmas Eve frantically searching for wing nuts and other critical parts, any other marital crisis will be a piece of cake.

The exercise machine arrived in a box containing what had to be thousands of parts. The instructions and parts list were the work of a sadist running wild. The assembly phase did not go well and, needless to say, it was several days before we could begin our exercise routine in earnest. A significant portion of the delay was the result of the machine itself. After being on the contraption for a few minutes, Margo had a nasty spill and a trip to the emergency room was necessary. Fortunately, she suffered only bumps and bruises and no severe lacerations. To use the machine effectively, one had to have the balancing ability of an acrobat, the coordination of a chimpanzee and the stamina of a marathoner. Simultaneously moving the arms and legs while trying to remain upright and breathe was a bit more difficult than we anticipated. Perhaps we became discouraged too easily but we soon sold the machine at a huge financial loss. Unfortunately, this was only the beginning.

Our thinking was that perhaps a machine which required the use of only one set of body parts at a time would be more to our liking. We were not built to use both arms and both legs in unison while attempting to remain in a vertical position. Hence, we settled on a tread mill, also built by the same company, Nordic Track. We did not realize that some tread mills have a motorized track which greatly reduces the effort necessary to make the mill operate. Instead, the machine we purchased required leg power of the participant to actually make the tread cycle around the rollers. In other words, a level of fitness, which we had not yet attained, was necessary in order to even use the machine right out of the box. If we already possessed that level of leg strength, we would have had no need for the tread mill in the first place. The engineers at Nordic Track had apparently put the cart before the horse, so to speak. After we sold this machine, we vowed never to purchase another exercise device from this particular company. We were of the opinion the company must have initially manufactured the machines found in torture chambers of long ago. Exercise machines were just a natural spin-off requiring the same type mind-set. The technology involved was exactly the same.

Over the next several years, we powered our way through a rowing machine, an exercise bike, a recumbent bike, a weight-lifting bench and equipment, and another type tread mill which we actually used, except for the three years it sat idle on our front porch. All these exercise machines, while vastly different, had one thing in common. They were sold for pennies on the dollar. This was in keeping with our long-standing policy to always buy high and sell low. Even though we have done this for years, it is not a practice we highly recommend because the obvious result is a negative cash flow. Based on our experience, there are probably more exercise machines sitting unused in American homes than the manufacturers would ever admit. They just keep churning them out and a gullible public scoops them up in a brief frenzy generally associated with a high school reunion. It is incredible at the variety of such devices on the market. What sort of twisted mind comes up with these things? There is no doubt this trend will continue until the much anticipated successful weight-loss pill comes on the market. Those already on the market do not work because we tried those in between our ill-fated exercise machine purchases.

Another factor all these devices have in common is the incredibly complicated assembly instructions. Generally, the first order of business is to ascertain whether or not all the necessary parts are present and accounted for. In order to accomplish this, the manufacturer suggests laying them out on the floor. It would take a floor the size of an aircraft hangar to spread all the items crammed into the boxes. Items such as bolt for right u shape bracket, front stabilizer end cap, screw ST4, curve washer for tension control knob, M10 nut for flywheel and sensor wire II L=1300 are such normal everyday items most of us can spot them easily enough. A major problem generally arises when I confuse the bolt for right u shape bracket with the bolt for left u shape bracket. It is difficult to believe, but occasionally screw ST2 is used instead of screw ST4 which negates hours of work. In order to simplify assembly, a parts drawing is included which is meant to show the purchaser how these parts fit together to form a completed product. Actually, it would make more sense if the manufacturer used ancient Egyptian hieroglyphics: it would make just as much sense to someone like me without an engineering degree.

Our most recent purchase of something called an elliptical included the following instructions:

Insert a ½" Bolt for left U Shape Bracket (13L) and put the Wave Washer (15) through the left U Shape Bracket (20). Put a Spring Washer (17) on the bolt, then pass it through the left Crank (75), and secure the bolt with a left nylon Nut (14L). Install one S13 Cap (28) onto the M845Bolt (23). Repeat this procedure for the right side assembly.

Please note: Before you put a Left nylon Nut (14L) and a Spring Washer (17) on the ½" Bolt for left U Shape Bracket (13L), make sure the ½" Bolt for left U Shape Bracket (13L) had been screwed to the end position with the left U Shape Bracket (20).

In order to install the hinge bolt properly, keep it perfectly straight when the bolt goes through the pedal tubing and the crankshaft. If the hinge bolt is connected to the crankshaft at an angle, damage to both the hinge bolt and the crankshaft may occur.

Important:

Please make sure the right bolt matches up with the right crank and the left bolt matches up with the left crank. If reversed the cranks may become damaged or stripped and the machine is rendered useless.

Attempting to decipher and follow correctly directions such as these may help explain the extremely high stress level experienced by many Americans. In the section labeled Product Safety, we are advised as follows: "If you feel any chest pains, nausea, dizziness, or shortness of breath, you should stop exercising immediately and consult your physician before continuing." In my case, these symptoms frequently occur while assembling the machine, not while exercising.

Since exercising at home did not turn out to be a really wise decision on our part, we turned instead to the exercise for profit side of the equation. At this point in our lives, our children were out of the house on their own and Margo had recently retired. The earlier constraints on time were gone. We focused our attention on a small gym nearby and soon became members under what was called their family plan. The relatively small space was chocked full of impressive looking machines which appeared to be really heavy and expensive. Thank goodness I wasn't responsible for assembling any of these monsters. In addition, there was a tanning room for members with an excessive dose of vanity and a shower for anyone who actually worked up a sweat.

We immediately found that the first order of business for new members was to receive intensive instruction on how to use the machines. This was not something to be taken lightly as we were to later discover. An abundance of warning labels attached to the devices explained why it was necessary for us to sign a form absolving the owner of any liability in the event we were injured or disfigured in any way while attempting to exercise. In spite of what most would consider adequate warning, in only a few days Margo managed to somehow get herself hopelessly entangled in one of the machines. It took me as well as the assistance of several complete strangers to finally extricate her without having to call 911. Thankfully, she was not injured, only humiliated. As a result of this embarrassing episode, her interest in the science of exercise soon waned and we allowed our family membership to lapse.

Years later, as a result of a shoulder injury, I had surgery to repair a torn rotator cuff. This particular injury was not the result of an over-zealous exercise routine on my part but was caused when a tree limb fell on my shoulder while cutting firewood. To the best of my memory, most of my physical injuries have been the result of carelessness on my part and not the handiwork of a passion to become physically fit. It should be obvious that I have never been that serious about exercising. The good people at the physical therapy center were tired of listening to me whine and whimper so they cut me loose as quickly as possible. The fact that my insurance coverage for therapy had been exhausted had absolutely nothing to do with me being dismissed from their care. They did appear to be rather eager to unload me on someone else so they recommended the YMCA as a solution for a stiff shoulder. Presumably, the large Olympic-size indoor pool would be just what the doctor ordered. My only experience with an indoor pool had been as a college freshman. All the good P. E. electives are already long-gone before freshmen have a chance to register and thus resulted in my forced enrollment in a swimming class. The only problem was that it was January and the water in the pool was not heated, only the air in the building. As a teenager I was foolish enough to go for a swim in spring-fed Cypress Creek in February and the water temperature was exactly the same as the indoor pool. Aside from a terminal case of blue lips and goose bumps, the only other problem was a mild bout with hypothermia.

Space in the Y pool to actually swim is about as rare as a politician willing to be hooked up to a lie detector. Waiting for a lane to open up was much worse than the waiting room at a doctor's office. In that setting, one can always peruse magazines that aren't quite as old as the printing press. However, at the Y, it was quite different. No matter the time of day, the pool was always occupied by large droves of women who could possibly have been infants when the printing press was invented. They never did really do any swimming in the true sense of the word, but only bobbed up and down like a fishing cork in rough water. It was bad enough on a normal day but when they all donned antlers at Christmas time it was more than I could stand. From my vantage point, they gave the impression of a herd of caribou swimming across the Bering Strait.

The large, airy room containing dozens of exercise machines was off limit to me. Since Margo and I had problems adjusting to similar machines earlier, I was honoring a self-imposed exile from any activity which might endanger my health or embarrass me publicly. Apparently, the Y staff had been trained to quickly call 911 at the slightest hint of a dues-paying member experiencing any type difficulty. The machines were the favorite of many very attractive younger females and they did not deserve to have to witness an old, fat, white guy being hauled away by emergency medical technicians. Therefore, with all my other options exhausted, I was forced to go to the upstairs walking track. Unfortunately, it overlooked the gym area where dozens of school-age kids were caged and engaged in games involving a lot of shouting and running. Soon, I was having flashbacks to my days as a junior high school teacher with playground and lunchroom duty. After months of mindlessly walking around the track with no end, I began asking myself: was this really a good use of my dues dollars? The obvious answer was a resounding, "No!"

After cancelling my membership, I hurried home and ordered a new elliptical machine. It may really be true that old habits are hard to break and few things in life ever actually change.

Jackie Hastings

This Old House

It might be a mite harsh and I don't mean to be overly critical but it has occurred to me that youth is wasted on young people. What a joy it would be to be young and actually comprehend those young years really are a gift from God. For many of us, when that realization does finally come, it is often paired with a face in the mirror we no longer recognize. I have tried valiantly not to lament the passing of those years but to smile because I had them for a while. Some of the fondest memories I have are the times spent in the old houses where I grew up. But maybe what all of us tend to call the old home place is not really a home after all but the people who occupied it with us. After all the supporting characters have moved on, it is pretty much impossible to ever go back home. We can go back to the old house that was once our home but it is not the same.

It is a wonderful blessing to be able to reflect back on a stable and supportive home. Sometimes I fail to realize many folks do not have fond memories like mine because they had no place they could really call home. My siblings and I share mostly wonderful memories of an old house in East Florence where they spent all their childhood and I spent most of mine until I was about fifteen. While this house holds a special place in my memories of home, there is another place I hold equally dear even though I spent far less time growing up there. I am referring to the house we began building in the country when I was only a boy and was not completely finished when I married and moved out as a young man.

It was always a dream for my daddy to move out of town. It is also special to me because I shared this dream with him and, for the most part, my daddy and I built most of the house, from foundation to roof line. The fact that I have a whole lot of what some people call "sweat equity" in the old house makes it even more special.

Daddy grew up dirt poor and spent his entire life working with his hands. Hard labor was all he knew and, at least to me, seemed to be his closest friend and constant companion. He made sure each of his children became acquainted with this old friend who still lingers in our memory, even today. The house we called home in East Florence had been pieced together from the original three-room wooden shack as Daddy came across enough building material to keep up with his steadily growing family. The old frame house was covered with tar paper which tried to give the appearance of brick but managed to fool no one. It was birthed as sort of a rectangular shape but morphed into something very odd with newer additions jutting out from both sides. People speak of the architectural style of their home as being ranch, colonial, western or any of a number of physical features which define the house in which they live. Our place was basically a tar paper shack which Daddy had improved over the years to become more presentable. When it was all over it provided a roof over the head of his seven children while at the same time providing a home for our grandfather and our mother's sister. Thankfully, we were rarely all present at the same time or we would have made the old woman who lived in a shoe look like the proverbial mansion on a hill.

My dad's mother died when he was only five years old and his raising was left to my grandfather, Jesse William McDonald, or Pa as he was called by all his grandchildren. Pa was sort of an iterant carpenter who traveled from job to job without a place of his own to call home. My daddy was his main helper and out of necessity learned to be a carpenter as well as anything else he was called upon to complete a job. At times Daddy's up-bringing was left in the hands of a lady he always referred to as Aunt Bummie. She was as close to a mother as he ever knew and loved her dearly. Aunt Bummie was actually Daddy's aunt on his mother's side of the family, Mary Frances Redding Rickard. Daddy's only surviving brother, Alphonse, was also farmed out by their father for friends and relatives to bring up and consequently the two brothers were raised in different homes by different families in the same community. Despite this separation, they remained very close and Uncle Alphonse's children, my cousins, and my brothers and sister were very close as well.

I remember my uncle Alphonse as a short, happy man who was a joy to be around and we all knew him as Uncle Doodle. For a period of time, Alphonse and his young family lived in a house built by my daddy out behind the old house we lived in. Daddy had originally built the house for my uncle Carlos and his wife. Uncle Alphonse moved his family in when our other uncle moved out. When they moved out, the house was torn down and the material was used to make our house larger. Daddy and Alphonse had a younger brother named Chalmus who died at the age of two. Their mother died only six months after Chalmus was born and thus began my daddy's saga of finding a place to call home. In the meantime, he could only follow his own father from job to job and house to house.

Daddy was determined to provide his children with a home and roots which he never enjoyed as a child. I have often heard that the two best things home can provide for a child is roots and wings. If that is true, he was successful. He and our mother struggled mightily during the years of the Great Depression and were forced to move from pillar-to-post to keep a roof over the head of their growing brood of kids and relatives. One of the earliest memories of my childhood was to hear Daddy talk of moving out of town to the country. He was convinced that hard times would soon be back and that living in the country would give his family a better opportunity to survive. He experimented with moving to a very isolated tract of land near Collinwood, Tennessee, for a short period of time before I was born but our mother would not hear of trying to raise a family so far from town and her parents. During this time he and some of my older brothers built a log cabin on the place which stands to this very day. As a matter of fact, my oldest brother, Bill, assigned me the task of determining if this dwelling was still in existence. I was happy to report to him before his death that, not only was it still standing, but I had pictures as proof.

As a boy I can vividly remember Saturday treks to the country with Daddy searching for a suitable, and affordable, piece of land on which to build the house my parents had cherished and dreamed of all their married lives. Some days it was a family outing and other times it was just me and my daddy. Over the years we must have looked at dozens of places but all were eventually rejected, most because of a very basic reason: a lack of money. After several years of futile searching, I began losing hope of ever living in the country but Daddy never stopped looking and dreaming.

Finally, when I was in the sixth grade, he paired up with my sister's husband and found a few acres of land in the Central community owned by Mr. Leo Burns. I was too young to be informed of the financial arrangements but because my wife and I later were blessed to call Leo our landlord, I can't help but believe the arrangement was one my daddy could afford. The land was purchased and split between Daddy and my sister and her husband. The tract of land was in use as a cornfield when it was purchased and because of this had absolutely no trees or shade of any kind. Today, it is covered with many huge trees most of which I planted as saplings. It is no longer recognizable as the desolate cornfield on a narrow dirt road from the late 1950's when we began the long drawn-out construction of our new home in the country.

My daddy's life-long dream began as nothing but an image in his mind and a strong back. My brother, Johnny, and I were the only boys left at home by this time as our brothers and sister had married and had families and worries of their own. Johnny and I were to form the nucleus and provide the labor for this project until he married and joined the Air Force in 1961. He was probably as determined to follow in the footsteps of all our brothers by joining the military as he was to remove himself from the labor intensive, do-it-yourself philosophy of our daddy. He never said and I never asked.

Daddy never embarked on a project of any kind that he didn't believe whole-heartedly he was capable of accomplishing by himself. Over the course of his life, he had picked up enough skill as a brick mason, plumber, electrician, roofer, sheet-rock finisher, and painter to go along with his skills as a master carpenter to do most anything he set out to do. A favorite story in our family was when our daddy, out of desperation, applied for a job as a sheet metal worker at TVA. He had absolutely no training or skill in that trade but told me that by the time they found out he was not a sheet metal worker, he would be the best one they had. Luckily for our family, he was hired and worked for TVA for almost thirty-five years. His sons benefitted from his jack-of-all trade's mentality by picking up enough skill in all these areas for each of us to become at least marginally proficient. Because of Daddy we believed, with some degree of confidence, we could do most anything we set our mind to do. As a matter of fact, my wife and I have been blessed to be able to build two new homes and I did much of the work myself: a chip off the old block.

This is not to say that all of us were willing volunteers but Daddy made it perfectly clear he did not run a debate club. Experience had taught all his children that Daddy did not tolerate slackers and it would be to our advantage to follow orders. During the course of my life I have actually witnessed children talking back to their parents and even refuse to do what they were told. It was an astonishing revelation to me that this type of behavior actually occurred on planet Earth. I believe I can safely say that none of W. E. McDonald's children were ever foolish enough to engage in behavior of this type. When our daddy gave us something to do we did it without any back talk. That is not to say we did it eagerly and it was often true we did have other, more pleasant, activities on our mind. The bottom line is that we understood the consequences and refusal was never an option. Daddy didn't raise a brood of angels by any means but he did raise a family that was not afraid of hard work. He served as judge, jury and executioner and was not real worried about due process rights of people he clothed, housed and fed. This was many, many years before parents began to be hauled into court for disciplining their children. Years before I was born, my brothers were instructed to dig a cellar under our old house using only picks, shovels and a wheel barrel. This old dirt cellar with a dirt floor and walls served for a few years as Daddy's workshop and storage area. It served for a much longer time as an interrogation room and dungeon where either a stern lecture or corporal punishment was meted out to those in need of a dose of reality. One or two trips to this cellar with Daddy were enough for him to persuade us it was not wise to get crossways with the head man. It seems to me that today many families do not know who is in charge and are rudderless. In order for a group of people to live together in close proximity someone must be in charge. In our family, that was my daddy. Many of those who seem intent on shunning gainful employment today would have benefitted greatly from being raised by my daddy. There is no doubt that much later in life his strict discipline and work ethic enabled each of us to better cope with making it in a difficult world. We grew to appreciate the lessons he set out to teach us.

The material used to build our new home in the country was hauled in a hand-made, bumper-pull trailer Daddy towed behind his car. He did not own a truck at that time in his life. We were never a two-car family because of the expense involved and the fact our mother never learned to drive. Every shovel of sand, bag of mortar, block, brick, piece of lumber of any size, nail, window, and roofing was hauled to the site in that little trailer. Daddy was not able to purchase anything in bulk. We were only able to work on the house on weekends and he purchased only enough material at a time to keep us busy for a couple of days. Also, he was wary of leaving material unprotected while we weren't on site. Maybe it was because of his very rough early life but Daddy was always suspicious of most people. He seriously suggested to my brother Bobby that he frisk a man he had working for him every day at quitting time to make sure he wasn't stealing any of his tools. My suggestion was this would do very little to foster a healthy employer-employee relationship and Daddy finally relented, but very reluctantly. As a result, he always owned a lot of padlocks and nothing was left unprotected, if at all possible. Needless to say, he carried a pistol with him every time we left the house.

Saturday was our big work day and we left home early. Our first stop was always at a building supply company in town for the needed materials for the day. We packed a lunch and took a cooler of water to last us until we returned to our house in town. As with all buildings, we began with the foundation. Most builders bring in a back-hoe for this task which usually takes only a few hours. We dug our foundation with a pick and shovel and it took literally months to remove the dirt and get the grading right working only on Saturdays. We hauled sand, gravel and bags of cement in order to mix the concrete to pour into the footing. There was no water on site so we also hauled a large, fifty gallon barrel of water to use with the concrete and mortar to lay the blocks. Daddy laid every block in the foundation while Johnny and I mixed mortar and carried the heavy blocks to where they were needed. After months of labor, we finally had the foundation to the point it was ready for the floor and this was cause for great celebration.

Before placing the wooden sills on the foundation, Daddy assigned me the task of coating each of the timbers with a layer of creosote to protect them from termites. Since it was summer, I worked without a shirt while painting the creosote on the wood which

34

was laid out on saw horses. Little did I know that working with the caustic creosote in the hot sun can burn the skin and I suffered greatly for a few days from that lethal combination of chemicals and the hot summer sun. Daddy was greatly disturbed because he felt it was his fault.

Not only did we not have water on site, neither did we have any electricity. Daddy grew up with a handsaw in his hand and taught each of us to use a saw long before we ever laid our hands on a power saw. As incredible as it seems, every board in that house from the foundation to the rafters was cut with a handsaw. Power did not arrive on site until the house was completely in the dry and we began working inside. Maybe this does not seem like a big deal to someone who has never been involved with building a house but, believe me, it is a very big deal. Houses today are built using power tools not even in existence during the early 1960's. It is unusual today to see a builder using a hammer, much less a handsaw. One of the reasons it took several years to move into the new house was the fact that every board had to be cut by hand. The subfloor and roof were not built by using the large sheets of plywood which cover a huge area. Instead, Daddy insisted on using individual planks for the floor and roof. Each one cut to size with a handsaw.

The last major outside task was to nail the shingles on the roof before moving inside. Naturally, we did it all ourselves with not a real roofer in sight. Roofing a house is extremely labor intensive and can be more than a miserable experience in very hot or very cold weather. The shingles have to be carried up a ladder, one heavy, awkward bundle at a time. Literally thousands of individual shingles have to be nailed in place one at a time with short roofing tacks. The very act of driving the tack exposes the fingers to severe abrasion from the gravel in the shingle and also creates the opportunity to pound fingers along with the wrong nail. Fingernails which have been shattered with a hammer will ache for days and throb with every heartbeat. Daddy solved this problem by drilling a hole in the fingernail with his pocket knife to release the bruised blood. It wasn't as painful as it sounds and it did bring immediate relief. In addition, skinned knees and a raw rear end are the inevitable result from scooting along the roof. All this is old news to anyone who has ever roofed a house.

Without recounting every nail driven, suffice it to say, it took a long time to get the house ready to occupy. It finally reached the point where we needed to move so that I could begin my high school years at Central. My brother Johnny graduated from Central after having transferred from the high school in Florence. It was a very long bus ride from our house in town because of so many stops and the bus having to turn around at the end of narrow dirt roads and driveways. As a result, we moved into the new house long before it was finished. The floors were plywood and none of the bedrooms or the bathroom had a real door, only a sheet hanging across the opening. The lack of doors, particularly on a bathroom, can cause real trauma for a teenage boy.

The long-awaited house in the country during the early 1960's.

As the house slowly crawled along to the point of being livable, one major, dreaded labor-intensive task remained. A septic system with field lines had to be installed and this grueling task is normally done with a back-hoe. Instead, Daddy assigned me the job of digging a pit large enough for a five hundred gallon concrete septic tank. So, with a pick and shovel, I began digging a hole which had to measure approximately seven feet deep, six feet long and five feet wide. He assured me the hole was already there, I just had to get the dirt out of it. The soil was largely clay-based and would fill up with water every time it rained. Daddy rigged up a hand operated pump which afforded me the additional task of pumping the water out before I could begin digging. After weeks of digging, Daddy finally relented and hired a guy to come in with a machine and complete the job. He was apparently afflicted with some sort of high fever which affected his thought process and resulted in a fit of leniency. However, the condition was only temporary and he did recover.

As with many things in life, our sojourn in our dream home in the country as a family did not last long. It was not one of those, "And they lived happily ever after," events. In just a little over two years after we moved my mother passed away and left just Daddy and me living there by ourselves. We never experienced the separation many teenage boys and their fathers go through and we remained very close. I can remember coming home late at night and the lights in the house would be a welcoming beacon at the end of a long drive way. One of the many things a home can provide is a light on a very dark night. Daddy may have dozed in his chair but he never went to bed until he knew I was safely back at home. My new wife and I moved into the house and lived there with him until our daughter was born. After we moved out, my daddy remarried and the house became the home of my brother Johnny and his family.

The same house as it appears today, more than fifty years later.

Currently, the old house which slowly came together raw and stark out of the stubble of a cornfield sits in a well-shaded yard and looks as if it had always belonged there and nowhere else. Time seems to do this with old buildings, especially homes where people have lived and shared the toils and hardships of life. My brother and his family improved the original house over the years and added a lot of grace and dignity to what it once was. After his death, his children, grandchildren and now great-grandchildren have made it a wonderful place to live. Four generations of the same family have now used it as a gathering place and it continues to thrive with life as only a family can bring to a house. Someday, it may well leave the family but that is the way with life, it moves on with us or without us.

The old house in East Florence has now been abandoned and it sits as an empty shell without even a spark of life. Age and decay are as destructive to old houses as they are to our earthly bodies. There comes a time when both reach the point of no return and life must go on. There is something extremely sad about a house that no longer serves as a home for a family. Occasionally, I will go out of my way just to drive by the old place and it is always a sad occasion. A house loses something when it has no family to keep it vibrant. Every old, abandoned house has a history which is known only to the people who once lived within its walls. People are like houses and even churches in a way: they are defined by the spirit of what lives inside and are much more than flesh, wood, stone and mortar. When the voices grow silent the spirit seems to disappear and its identity is lost in a world that has no time to care or remember. The first verse and chorus of an old song entitled, *This Old House*, pretty well sums it all up:

> This old house once knew my children,
> This old house once knew my wife.
> This old house was old and comfy as we fought the storms of life.
> This old house heard many laughter this old house heard many shouts.
> Now it trembles in the darkness as the lighting rolls about.

> Ain't gonna need this house no longer,
> Ain't gonna need this house no more.
> Ain't got time to fix the shingles,
> Ain't got time to fix the floor.
> Ain't got time to oil the hinges,
> Nor to mend the window panes.
> Ain't gonna need this house no longer,
> I'm getting ready to meet the Saints.

In spite of the fact that my daddy's dream of living in the country as a family was short-lived, much of my life has been impacted by those few years together in our new home. If we had continued as before and remained in town, my life would have been drastically changed. I would never have enrolled in the school where I met my future wife. Friends who have enriched my life would be total strangers to me as I would be to them. My family as I know it today would not exist. The church down the road from our old house would not have become a major part of my life for over fifty years. Without the love and support of a church family there remains the very real possibility I would have never made the life-changing decision to accept Christ as my Savior.

No decision is ever made in a vacuum and the reverberations can continue for generations in a family. The fact is that outside of a few obvious facts we will never know the full extent of what might have been. I have a lot to be grateful for in my life and at the top of the list is the fact that my daddy had a dream which changed more lives for the better than he could possibly have ever known.

Pig Tales

It doesn't take a genius to realize how different things are today than in times past. Events that are commonplace and readily accepted today were totally unheard of in the 1950's and the 1960's. It would take a fellow a long time to make a list of all the changes over the years, some of them good, some not so good and some of them just downright bad. Luckily, my memory fails me and most of them cannot be recalled from the dark recesses of my brain.

One change in particular which comes to mind that is both good and bad is the incredible dependence we have today on the computer. There is no doubt that computers have made a tremendous improvement in the fields of communication, medical science, travel and so many other areas they are too numerous to count. There is also no doubt that computers can instantly bring incredible evil right into our own homes in the form of porn and child predators. Like many other advances over the years, we have not yet learned to harness only the good and eliminate the bad that always seems to accompany technological changes. I still have trouble figuring out why I can't buy a gallon of gas or a loaf of bread when the computers are down. That makes no sense!

Another negative is that items we purchase are packaged so securely that one needs a chain saw in order to remove the wrapping. In many cases, the wrapping dwarfs the item it purports to protect. Furthermore, once we gain entry, the item inside may not even work properly and that only adds to the frustration. As a nation we may have fallen behind other countries in certain areas but Americans can package an item better than anybody in the world, even the Chinese. An oyster shell has nothing on a bottle of aspirin when it comes down to getting to what is inside.

One thing I have noticed is that children have no clue where the food, particularly meat, originates that is brought home from the grocery store. Kids in school actually have to go on field trips in order to lay their eyes on a real pig or cow or chicken. A while back, Margo and I went to a farm to purchase some pumpkins for fall decorating. A group of school children were there and I heard one of the boys shout to a friend, "Look, a real chicken." In a very indirect way that brings me to the subject of the role of pigs in today's world.

Today, pigs are big, in more ways than one. At this point it might be a good idea if all the vegetarians move on to other, less offensive, reading material. I have always been fond of pigs mostly because I enjoy pork chops, ham, sausage, bacon and, yes, even pickled pigs' feet. There are few things more enjoyable than waking up to the smell of a pig frying: hopefully, of course, in the form of ham or bacon on the stove early in the morning. Believe it or not, there is one thing about pigs that I simply cannot stomach, so to speak. That is the odd attraction some people have for pigs that necessitates keeping them in their homes as pets. Folks, God did not create pigs in order for them to become pets. Pigs are actually riding around in cars, waddling along city streets on a leash and appearing regularly on television shows as guests. This is not natural and only offers more evidence that our society has degraded to the point of no return. What is the world coming to? At this point, I must confess to a lifelong association with pigs but, thankfully, never to the point of even considering keeping one in the house.

My first full scale contact with pigs came when I was around ten years old. My dad and oldest brother, Bill, who was married and owned several acres of land out of the city limits, went together and bought four pigs of about thirty pounds each. They intended to raise the pigs and then slaughter them for use by our family. By this I mean we intended to kill and eat them hence, another very good reason not to become close friends with a pig. We built a pen and adequate shelter a short distance from my brother's house and, presto, we were in the pig business. Every afternoon for several months my daddy, my brother Johnny, and I drove the few miles from our house in East Florence to the pig pen, bringing feed and water to the critters.

All of this took place during the mid-1950s, and every house in our community had a slop bucket hanging somewhere outside. Obviously, this extremely messy container was not kept real close to the house, but far enough away to avoid the flies and smell. This bucket was the repository for food wastes from the kitchen table, if the family owned no pigs or pets to consume it. There was no garbage collection in our community and most everyone burned what they could, or deposited it in a deep ditch, and saved the table scraps in their slop bucket. Daddy had arranged with several of our neighbors for us to collect the scraps to feed to our small herd of pigs. This practice is now against government regulations so today's swine have to be content with grain and cannot enjoy corn bread, beans, tomatoes and other delicacies. This regulation, among millions of others, supposedly protects people but it is possible the government has something against pigs enjoying a good meal.

When I say, "for us to collect the scraps," I am actually referring to my brother and me. Our daddy did not stoop to this level. This was accomplished by periodically creeping furtively around to the neighbor's back yard and emptying their slop bucket into our larger bucket. This was only one of many jobs our daddy assigned to us to help build our character. His policy was to start at the bottom and work your way up the ladder. A collector of slops was about as low a rung on the ladder as we could go and anything else would have to be considered a move toward the top. This explains why we were lurking behind the houses instead of marching boldly and proudly through the front yards. As you can imagine, emptying our neighbors' slop buckets was not something we bragged about to our friends and this particular training never appeared on a resume we might have submitted for employment. But, as it is so often said about other not so glamorous jobs, somebody has to do it. So, Johnny and I collected the table scraps and rode with them in the trunk of Daddy's car to keep the slop from splashing and turning over to our brother's house. Today, I am positive that two small boys in the trunk of an old Packard automobile, with the lid open and holding five gallon buckets of slop would attract the attention of the authorities and our daddy would be deprived of free labor for a good while. As a matter of fact, he would be the one supplying the free labor while he served a stint in jail.

Since there were six boys in our family, our daddy thrived on free labor. If he couldn't find something to keep us busy at home he would loan us out to neighbors who also thrived on free labor. Over the years, my brothers and I spent many valuable Saturdays pulling nails from used lumber, cleaning up used bricks and generally making ourselves useful for the benefit of a neighbor whose children left town with the circus to escape working for nothing. In college I learned that it is unlawful to even loan prisoners out as sort of slave labor but that information came along too late for me or any of my brothers. To tell the truth, many of my dad's child-rearing practices have been called into question recently by the authorities charged with preventing the exploitation of children.

Anyway, back to the pigs. Daddy mixed the slop with what he called shorts which were pellets of ground grain bought at the feed store. Many might find this surprising but there is something very satisfying about watching pigs while they are eating, especially when they are eating slop out of a wooden trough. However, this might not be universally true and it could be an acquired preference. If the bureaucrat who decreed swine could no longer eat food scraps could actually watch them eating, he would realize he was depriving pigs of one of the few joys of their generally very short lives. A lot of valuable life lessons can be learned by observing this process. The term our mother used to describe a table full of kids was, "don't eat like a pig." Actually, she meant this as a way to embarrass us but the pigs would have been embarrassed if they were somehow forced to watch us eat. Also, the term, "eating at the high end of the trough," shed new light on the plight of the poor pig stuck on the upper end as all the semi-liquid slop ran to the lower

43

end. Our household was very large and included not only my siblings and parents but frequently extended family as well. Being stuck at the high end of the trough was a term the youngest and smallest of a large family would appreciate.

Like many people, a pig never seems satisfied with his station at the trough. No matter where he is, he always wants the place of the pig next to him and there is a constant effort to push the other pigs out of the way. Humans and pigs seem to have more in common than a heart valve, which is remarkably similar. In case the reader didn't know, this valve is frequently used in humans to replace worn out heart parts and has prolonged the life of thousands of people. So, providing a very satisfying meal is not the only contribution swine have made to mankind.

Raising hogs for meat involves more than food and water. There are many other, mostly unpleasant, chores associated with keeping a bunch of pigs. The tusks of a young pig must be trimmed and their snout is frequently pierced with a ring-like device which deters them from "rooting-up" the ground. This for the hogs is the only way to locate edible roots since a shovel was out of the question. This brings to mind another phrase of my childhood, "root hog or die." It was generally heard something like this, "Son, it's time to root hog or die." Most often it was directed at shiftless people who did not want to work for a living. If they weren't willing to change their ways then life was going to get really bad.

Probably the most unpleasant task involving hogs is a surgical procedure which is sometimes simple and sometimes not so simple. A male hog with all his male parts is called a boar. A male human being with all his male parts can also be called a "bore" but it is very different. Boars grow up to be somewhat testy, and not very tasty if they are still in possession of vital reproductive organs. After the successful removal of these parts, the aforementioned boar is now called a shoat. A shoat is good for only one thing, the dinner table and I don't mean as an invited guest. In order to eliminate the tough, strong taste, the boar has to have these parts removed; preferably at a very young age. Holding a twenty pound pig for this procedure is much easier than holding a hog that weighs a hundred pounds or so. Being novices in the swine business, we did not realize this essential fact until it was too late. The cute, baby pigs had, within a few months, reached a size that holding them was not only difficult, but dangerous.

My dad was a carpenter at TVA and worked with a fellow with the first name of Floyd. I knew Floyd reasonably well because he came by our house often. He was a big fellow and was always brimming with confidence and full of tall tales. Floyd was particularly impressed with his own physical strength and made no bones about it. No matter what story someone else told, Floyd could always top it with one of his own. His tales always mesmerized me until the day I heard him tell my dad he had killed a rattlesnake that was twelve inches between the eyes. I wasn't real familiar with rattlesnakes, but I had caught dozens of black snakes, chicken snakes and their other non-poisonous cousins and I knew that a snake measuring twelve inches between the eyes might be possible but only in the deep jungles of Africa, not in Lauderdale County. From that day forward I was of the opinion that Floyd was full of it and his credibility with me was shot.

Well, it seems that Floyd had guaranteed my dad that he, all by himself, could hold the hogs while my dad performed the required surgical procedure. I believe he said it would be, "a piece of cake." The event was scheduled for a Saturday and I, as any boy normally would, eagerly anticipated being a spectator, in the same vein as the Romans and gladiators. Blood and gore are fascinating to boys as long as it belongs to someone else and is viewed from a safe distance. I was all for learning about new things and was positive none of my friends had ever witnessed such an occurrence. This one singular event would give me bragging rights for weeks, and maybe months.

The night before, my dad painstakingly sharpened his pocket knife on the whetstone he kept in his secret box at home. Dad kept what I called his secret box stashed away in the lower corner of a closet. It was a long metal box which he kept padlocked. Everyone knew there was to be no tampering with that box and the contents were, indeed, mostly a secret. At times he would let me sit and watch in awe as he opened the box. To me, this was far more exciting than the opening of King Tut's tomb was to a bunch of archaeologists. I know for a fact Daddy kept a loaded .45 caliber Army pistol, the whetstone and some insurance policies in the box. Insurance agents would regularly come by our house to collect the premiums and Daddy would get the papers out of the box. We were never privy to what else was in the box and knew better than to ask. Today, his secret box sits empty in my workshop and I am still reluctant to open it.

The day of the big event dawned and we were there on site bright and early. My dad was never late for anything and he passed that trait down to most of his children. However, one brother and my only sister failed to grasp the concept of being on time and they have never been bothered by the fact that people were kept waiting because of their tardiness, but this information is not relevant to this particular story. My dad and Floyd had a plan for the task at hand but it was not a good plan. Experience has taught me that a bad plan is sometimes worse than no plan at all. Theoretically, Daddy, his friend Floyd along with my brother Bill would corner the pigs and then Floyd would sort of bulldog the closest pig like a cowboy bulldogging a steer at the rodeo. Dad would then jump in with a razor sharp KaBar knife; whack, whack, then bring on the next pig. Bill's job was to quickly apply a foul smelling, homemade concoction to the incision to keep flies out of the wound. One might assume that by this time the pig had lost whatever dignity he might have but this was not the case. Upon application of this compound, the pig apparently thought his rear end had been set ablaze and momentarily forgot about the parts he had left behind. Upon being released, his rear end immediately dropped to the ground and slid the entire length of the pen as the poor creature sought to put out the fire. I wasn't real sure about re-incarnation but I knew I didn't want to return as a pig.

They say that the best battle plans quickly disappear in what is called, the, "fog of war." Floyd's plan suffered the same fate. The bulldogging event at a rodeo is feasible only because the steer has a neck. The cowboy leaps from his horse, grabs the steer by the horns, digs in his heels to bring the animal to a halt, twists the scrawny neck until the steer falls down and , presto, the event is over, bring on the next steer. Keep in mind the fact they never use strong powerful bulls with heavily muscled necks in this event. Twisting the neck is crucial. As I remember the event, one of Floyd's biggest mistakes was his failure to take into account the fact that a pig basically has no neck. His large, melon-sized head is attached directly to his shoulders and is armed at one end by a mouth full of extremely sharp teeth. There is no scrawny neck to twist to bring a pig to the ground. Come to think of it, I have never seen a pig stand and look behind him by turning his head as a horse or cow might be prone to do. That feat is impossible to accomplish without a neck. Another grievous mistake was that Floyd had also failed to anticipate the foot speed of a pig. They are actually very fast critters over a short distance, as anyone who has ever been chased by a pig will attest. A nearby tree, which can be climbed rather quickly, is always a good thing to have nearby when fooling around with swine, domestic or feral.

As my dad and Floyd pursued the panicked swine around the pen, the poor pigs stampeded from one corner to the other until they were simply exhausted. Realizing his opportunity was finally at hand, Floyd grabbed a pig and attempted to bulldog the critter. He did manage to get the pig in a head lock but could not bring it to a stop. When building the pen, my brother and Daddy cleverly lined the inside with old, rusted metal from a long- gone barn. This was done to prevent the pigs from rooting under the wire and escaping. It did prevent the pigs from getting their nose under the wire but it presented a real hazard for Floyd. He was, unfortunately, trapped between the terrified pig and the rusty metal as it barreled around the pen, running as close to the perceived safety of the fence as possible. Floyd's body served as sort of a bumper and did prevent the pig from being cut badly but, unfortunately, Floyd suffered some nasty lacerations and bruises for his effort.

Daddy had warned me and my brother to stay out of the pen and keep out of the way. Daddy's warnings were never idle threats so we were more than glad to obey, considering the ruckus that was playing out before our very eyes. However, as the pig made one of many circuits of the pen with Floyd on his neck and Daddy and Bill hanging on to the rear, he shouted, "You boys get in here and help Floyd hold this pig!" Apparently his concern for our well-being was waning rapidly with each trip around the pen. You see, Floyd was still trying to flip the pig over on its side so Daddy could, in polite terminology, "fix" the pig. Two physical features make it virtually impossible to get a pig on its side: an extremely low center of gravity and short, stubby, stout legs. I wasn't sure what contribution my eighty pounds of weight, devoid of any muscles to speak of, could make but Johnny and I quickly entered the fray. Since Floyd was hanging to the front end and Daddy and Bill to the rear end, we could see no other choice than to jump astride the critter and ride him into the ground. Johnny grabbed ahold somewhere toward the rear. Trying to ride a pig is sort of like trying to ride a barrel because there is nothing to hang onto. There is an old saying that describes something that is of absolutely no value as, "worthless as a side saddle on a hog." Actually, a side saddle would have come in handy that day but, mercifully, it was a very short ride. The only thing that brought this ridiculous scene to a halt was sheer exhaustion on the part of the pig. This poor animal was dragging a very large man which had it in a headlock, and another much smaller man holding onto its' tail. To make matters even worse, two rather skinny boys were now on its' back and holding on for dear life. The beast finally decided that surrender was his only option. He quietly sank to his knees and the dirty deed was accomplished in a few short seconds. This insane scenario was repeated three more times before the day was over, although the three remaining pigs were about tuckered out by the time their surgical procedure was scheduled and didn't offer as much resistance. Bill poured the vile mixture of turpentine and other noxious chemicals on the incision to keep the flies away and this gave the pigs another brief burst of energy as they ran away with their rear end scooting along on the ground. Johnny and I agreed later, privately of course, that it was not wise to apply any kind of a fiery concoction to this area of the anatomy.

The pigs finally retreated to the far corner of their pen and stayed there for several days, too exhausted and sore to move, probably thinking their worst nightmare was now over. Little did they know about hog killing time that was yet to come.

Daddy had started his family during the 1920's and suffered mightily during the worst years of the Great Depression. Consequently, he refused to throw away anything edible. My wife finds it amusing that I actually eat the end pieces of a loaf of bread and scrape the bottom of peanut butter and mayonnaise jars. Old habits are hard to break. Anyway, our family, or, at least, some of us, enjoyed our first meal of fried mountain oysters that night for supper.

Those who can remember hog killing time recall it as a day of great excitement in a family. If the timing was right, the pigs penned up during the summer have become fully grown hogs and would reach killing size, about three hundred pounds, by the beginning of winter. Hog killing had to occur on a day when it was cold enough to keep the spoiling process at bay for a few hours while the meat was being cut and salted on outside tables set up for the occasion. Thus, the origin of another term, "It's cold enough to kill hogs."

Much preparation was necessary before this day arrived. Wood had to be cut and stacked and water hauled for the barrel in which the carcass was dipped to loosen the hair. Knives were sharpened and salt purchased to begin the curing process. The great majority of the meat had to be preserved by salting and smoking to last through the winter months. Refrigeration was available but the average refrigerator, or ice box, as we called them for years, was very small and not suitable for meat storage. It wasn't unusual for neighbors to drop by to help because they knew their pay would be several pounds of fresh pork for the table.

As a small boy I was of little use in the heavy lifting of hog killing, of which there is a lot associated with the task. My job was mainly to go retrieve anything Daddy needed and to keep the fire burning under the barrel. Dipping a three hundred pound hog carcass into a barrel of hot water was not an easy undertaking because it had to be retrieved out of the barrel at just the right time. If allowed to stay in the hot water too long the hair is virtually impossible to remove. I remember how clean the white skin of the Yorkshires looked hanging from a tree limb after the hair had been removed. Daddy cut each side away from the backbone with a meat saw, which was simply a giant hacksaw, and lifted the loin out of the backbone. If the loin is left inside the backbone, it is cut up and becomes the meaty part of a pork chop. One of Daddy's favorite sayings was that he used every part of the hog except the squeal and he really did. He used the jowl from the head to cook with black-eyed peas to eat on New Year's Day. This tradition remains in my family even today and I do not ever remember a New Year's meal without black-eyed peas and hog jowl. Supposedly it brings good luck and who knows what would have happened had we given up the practice. The remainder of the head was boiled until all the meat

48

loosened from the bone and was pressed into lengths called, appropriately, head cheese or souse meat. This was strictly an acquired taste and looked something like modern day Spam, only a lot greasier. Daddy sliced it for sandwiches to take to work. The choice cuts like the ham, shoulder, and bacon were salted down and kept in the salt box for several weeks until they were needed as is or hung in the smokehouse for the drawn out smoking process.

At this point in my life my association with swine, of the four footed variety, sort of plateaued and contact was at a minimum, except at the breakfast or dinner table. When I accepted a teaching position after college it became necessary to find a part-time job, as it still is with many male teachers, to support my growing family. My wife and I had purchased several acres of land with plenty of running water and I had fenced it and built a barn for my horse. The time was right for me to get into the hog business in a big way, sort of.

Topping hogs out to slaughter size of about two hundred fifty pounds requires a lot of money, labor and equipment. However, running a few sows and a boar to raise feeder pigs was something a fellow could start off small and build over time. The feeder pigs were then purchased at a sale and raised to slaughter size. My first investment was to buy six gilts, young female swine, and then raise them to breeding age. A neighbor loaned me the use of his old boar and I was off and running in the pig business. To my credit, I was smart enough not to wait until my pigs were large enough to ride before the necessary work was done on them. At about two weeks of age I "fixed" each male, clipped all their tails and snipped the two teeth that would eventually become tusks if allowed to grow. Thankfully, Floyd's help was not required. The object was to raise pigs to about fifty pounds each and then sell them at a sale in a small town about thirty miles away. My first litters did not sell well and I was advised to buy a good quality boar. Breeding age boars were too expensive for my fledgling operation so, instead, I bought a two month old registered Duroc boar. This breed is characterized by their long, lean body and red color. He grew into as fine a boar as one could want and was also as friendly as a lap dog in a nursing home. The quality of my feeder pigs improved tremendously, with Red's able assistance and I found that raising feeder pigs was something I really enjoyed.

My sweet wife, bless her heart, in her never-ending and unfailing efforts to cover for her husband's shortcomings, had an encounter with the red boar which still provides a lot of laughs. At maturity he weighed a good three hundred pounds and occasionally allowed me a good natured ride around the barn yard, without the side saddle of course. A major drawback to keeping animals of any kind is the problem of keeping them contained inside a fence. Like many people I know, most animals prefer to live on the other side of the fence. They say the grass is always greener on the other side but it has to be something else. Some animals are more difficult to keep fenced in than others and goats are the number one offender in my book. The only way a goat will stay confined is if it suits him at the moment. Hogs are not as difficult but they sometimes come in a close second. Our place bordered Cypress Creek which was an excellent source for fresh water. The fence extended a few yards out into the creek but the big boar enjoyed the cool water and sometimes emerged from the creek on the wrong side of the fence. This error gave him free run of a huge creek bottom until we could find him and bring him back home. He turned up missing one Fall day and one of our neighbors on the creek called and said he was behind her house. This happened several times but he was always gone by the time I arrived on the scene. One day, while I was at work, Margo called me and told me the boar was once again at our neighbors and wondered what to do. Following my sage advice, she trudged down into the creek bottom armed only with a bucket of shelled corn. The boar was well versed in being fed and would follow a feed bucket most anywhere. The plan worked fine but Margo had to occasionally halt and allow the hog to stop and get his bearings. He was apparently intoxicated from eating fermented wild plums, apples and muscadines off the ground for almost a week. He would follow the bucket for a few steps before he had to stop and sit down on his haunches. A few grudging steps at a time, Margo led the large, red boar out of the creek bottom and up the hill to the pasture gate. What a woman!

This was not the only episode that showed what a really good woman I had chosen to be my wife. During the summer I was in graduate school out of town and during the school year I took some courses at a local university as a transfer student. This unfortunate turn of events placed a lot of the care and responsibility on my wife, Margo. She was very frank and up front about the whole situation and told me to my face that she did not like pigs or hogs and frequently harbored bad feelings toward anyone who did. However, being the jewel of a wife that she was, she fed the animals on those afternoons I was in class. Feeding a bunch of large sows is a chore in itself and doing it in the winter makes it even worse. It seems that she would frequently get between the sows and the feed trough, not a good idea, and the sows would sort of knock her around in their haste to get at the meal. On a few occasions, she would find herself riding on the back of one when it ran between her legs. While I would have loved to witness this, I knew not to laugh because I was already on thin ice.

Our marriage almost suffered a fatal blow one summer when I was away at school and my crop of feeder pigs had reached prime weight. Waiting until the next sale would put them over weight and they would bring a much lower price. My most persuasive powers were put to a stern test trying to convince her to load the pigs in my old pickup and drive them to the feeder pig sale. The line of trucks and trailers waiting to unload grew longer as the morning progressed and it was not good to let pigs stay in the back of a hot truck during the heat of the day. Swine cannot sweat and frequently die of heat stress. Most of the time when I took pigs to the sale I left the night before and slept in the truck cab so I could unload early. Out of her never ending, well, almost never ending, love for me she agreed but was not happy at all. Considering all the bad things that could have happened the day went well for Margo and the pigs. Daddy helped her load the pigs and it was during the loading process that Margo heard my dad use his first curse word in her presence. Much to his dismay, he let a bad word slip out because enticing a couple dozen pigs to run up a ramp into the bed of a truck is sort of like trying to hem in quicksilver, if you know what I mean. Dad's confidence level around pigs had suffered a major blow years earlier when he and Floyd had such a difficult time trying to castrate much larger hogs. He was never able to fully recover.

My dad had always treated Margo like royalty and he loved her as much as any of his own children. As a kid, I often heard him weave together strings of profanity that would have made a drunken sailor envious. To his credit, he never cursed around his daughters-in-law and stopped completely when he found the Lord later in life. To have been a fly on the wall, so to speak, and watch my dear wife, not only load the pigs but waiting in line at the sale barn with all the guys in overalls, spitting tobacco juice would have been a joy to behold. Even better, would have been watching her back the truck up to the unloading dock so that the gate on the rear of the truck was lined up with the gate to the holding pen. Backing a vehicle is one of the very few things my wife does not do well. I figured that if she wanted me to know all the details she would tell me sooner or later, but she never did. But, there are times in all our lives when we have to learn not to put into words all the crazy thoughts that rattle around in our head. Every opinion that enters our brain does not automatically meet all the standards necessary to pass through our lips as a sentence. For the benefit of everyone concerned, there are times when we just have to keep our mouth shut.

My days in the pig business are long past and seem like they belong in another life. Virtually all the pork raised today comes from mega farms which are multi-million dollar operations. But that doesn't keep me from smacking my lips when I smell bacon frying on the stove.

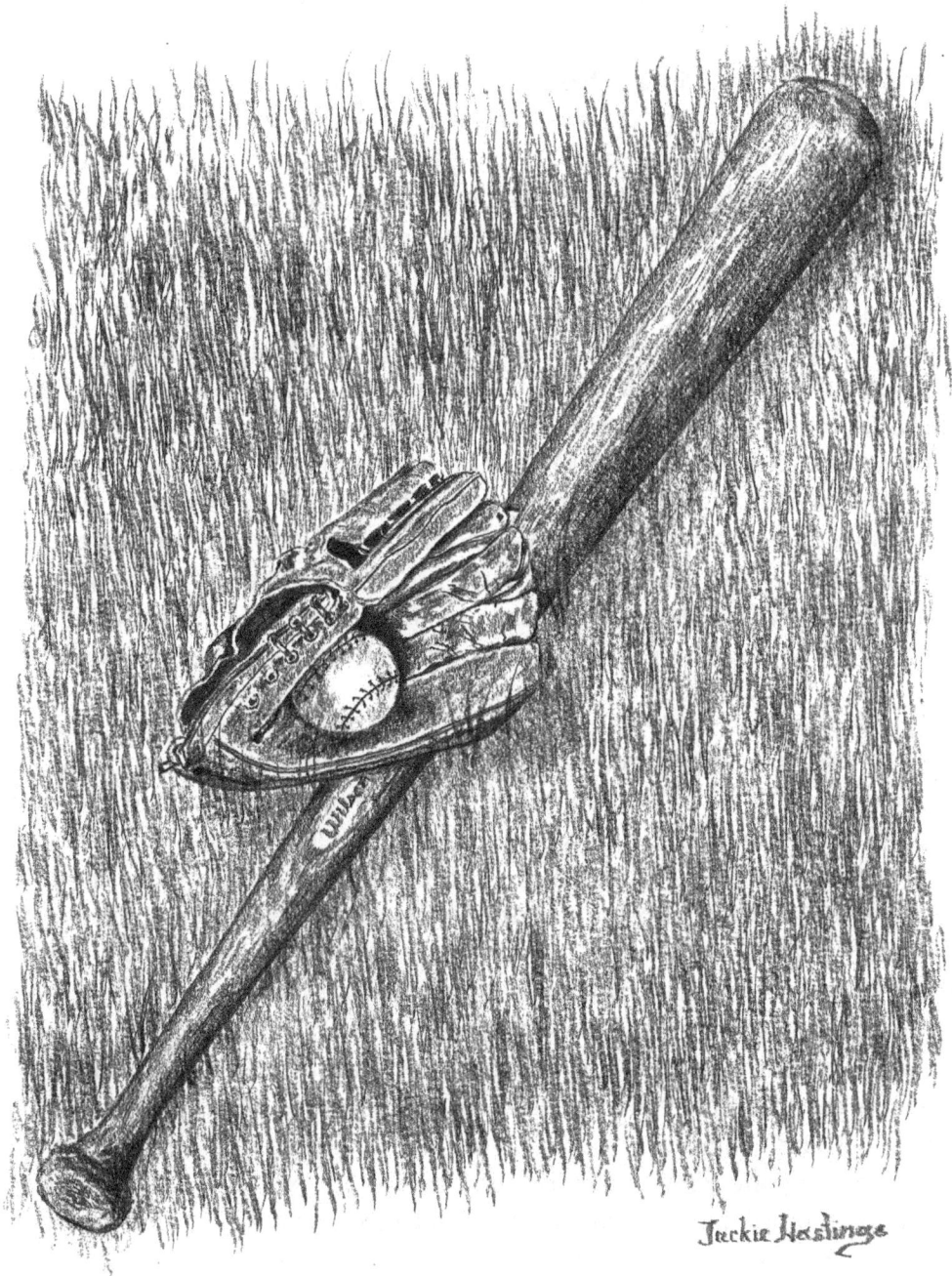

Jackie Hastings

Baseball Memories

I stood for hours at a time in front of the brick wall separating our yard from our neighbors. Their house was on the side of the hill a little higher than ours and my dad built the wall to separate the two yards. Whatever the purpose, it served as a handy way to practice fielding ground balls when I was old enough to throw a baseball. A thrown ball hit the wall and bounced back with enough speed to provide a boy the rare opportunity to practice baseball by himself. As I grew older and stronger I practiced forehand and backhand fielding techniques and tried to hit a certain spot on the wall with my throw. Unfortunately, the potted geranium plants Mrs. Rosie Jones, our neighbor's mother-in-law, always kept sitting on top of the wall frequently suffered greatly from the many errant throws on my part. The countless broken flower pots were sufficient evidence that being a pitcher was not in my future. My intention was to recompensate her for the lost pots when I was playing second base for the New York Yankees. However, an inability to hit the curve ball and being extremely slow afoot kept me, among many other liabilities, from achieving my boyhood dream. Each time I broke one of her pots I would religiously go to her and apologize and she would always tell me it was okay. Thank goodness for good neighbors and a grand lady who understood a little boy and his love for baseball.

As I grew older I was able to graduate from my brick wall and playing catch with my dad to actually playing sandlot games with the other kids in the community. Just the same, playing catch with my dad was something I never grew tired of and will always remember with fond memories. As a matter of fact, if I had the opportunity today to go back in time and do one thing I really enjoyed, it would be playing catch with my dad in the yard. There is something about a son or daughter and their dad just tossing around a baseball. It wasn't until I was a father myself and came home tired and wanted to do nothing more than plop myself down on the couch and rest that I fully understood the situation. Despite being extremely tired from working all day, my dad was always willing to go out in the yard with me and "play catch" as I would say. No matter how much wealth a man might accumulate during his life it will never be enough to make up for not spending time with his children. A man who will not take the time to play catch with a son or daughter is missing one of the great joys of fatherhood. Not only that, he is depriving his children of a memory they will take with them to their grave. I cherished this opportunity with my own children just as I cherished it with my dad.

One of the grandest days of my life was when Dad took me and my brother Johnny to Hibbett's Sporting Goods when it was in its original location downtown. It was located on Court Street next door to my uncle Hardy Springer's Gulf station. My mother's sister, Carmel, was married to a fellow by the name of Hardy Springer who was a nice enough guy but known as a skinflint of the worst order. My aunt Carmel was called Sister Springer by all who knew her, friends and relatives alike. This seems rather odd to me today but back then it seemed perfectly normal. My aunt and uncle had one child who lived out of town and our aunt was fearful of staying home alone so she frequently just sat at the gas station all day. If the truth were told, she was a very lonely lady. My mother and father preferred to visit her at the station because my aunt had a lot of peculiar ways. Inviting others to her home was one of the most noticeable. On these dreaded occasions our parents would always grab up what kids were around at the time and drag us along. Being the youngest, I was always around. Our dad must have understood what an ordeal it was for us to just sit so he often allowed Johnny and me to go to the sporting goods store next door and look around during the interminably long visits by our parents. We never had the money to buy anything but just the opportunity to smell the leather gloves and see rows and rows of bats and new, white baseballs was a visual and sensory feast. One particular time was different because Daddy told us to pick out a brand new glove. It was sort of baffling because it was not Christmas and birthdays were never big at our house. Birthdays were so insignificant at our house Daddy never had a clue when any of his children's birthday came around. It is not a good idea to look a gift horse in the mouth so we plunged into the stock of new gloves like a woman at a shoe sale. We had never had a new glove and had to share one, handed down from a series of older brothers. The old family heirloom had been patched and re-patched so many times it was hardly recognizable as a glove. Johnny picked out a Rawlings and my choice was a Nokona. In my immature kid brain I knew for a fact that my dad had just punched my ticket to New York. A brand new glove would make my move to the Yankees a slam dunk certainty. There was no doubt by the time Bobby Richardson retired I would be ready to take his place at second base. However, a new glove does nothing for a poor hitter and a runner with the foot speed of a sloth. The day I was able to buy my very first new Silverado pickup, some fifty-five years later, pales in comparison to the day my daddy bought me a brand new baseball glove. Be that as it may, I used this new glove from that point through high school: hopefully fielding more grounders than I booted.

During the early 1950's there was no such thing as televised baseball games. For us, that was a moot point because we did not own a television. However, we did own the world's largest radio. This monstrosity sat in our living room and was large enough for a family of six to use as a kitchen table or possibly a dance floor. It had what seemed like dozens of knobs and literally hundreds of the old style vacuum tubes and took a really long time to warm up. When it reached full strength the old radio sort of glowed and emitted a lot of heat as well as a strange humming noise. However, the radio did allow us to listen to the Birmingham Barons play baseball. Their opponents were the Memphis Chicks, Atlanta Crackers, Little Rock Travelers, New Orleans Pelicans, Chattanooga Lookouts, Nashville Vols and the Knoxville Smokies, all members of the old Southern League. Of course, these were all minor league teams but baseball was baseball and it was all we had. I suppose we picked Birmingham because of geography and we listened religiously along with our dad who was actually a real fan of baseball. For some reason we sort of chose a catcher by the name of Johnny Blanchard as our idol. He was born in Minneapolis and threw right and batted left. It is amazing what kids can absorb when involved with something interesting.

If the game on the radio continued past our bedtime, Daddy sent us to bed but kept the volume loud enough for us to listen from our bedroom. Johnny and I shared a very small room which was not much larger than a closet. Daddy did not believe in spending money on such frivolous items as furniture so our room had a built-in bed, two built in desks and a place to put our clothes. The bed was basically a wooden platform with a box spring and a mattress on top. We had agreed early on to share the bed equally so there was an imaginary line drawn right down the middle which could not be crossed by either party after we were officially in bed. One day, desperate for a comic book fix, I sold Johnny twelve inches of my side of the bed for one thin dime. It didn't take long for me to realize the error of my ways. If the federal government enforced our nation's borders in the same fierce manner my brother kept me off my former space, there would be no immigration problem. It was as if he never slept. During the middle of the night I would be rudely awakened anytime an errant arm or leg accidentally crossed over the imaginary line onto his side. The term buyer's remorse was not yet a part of my world but I certainly had a bad case of seller's regret. Be that as it may, we listened to the game until it ended or our dad turned the radio off and went to bed.

Not until much later in life did I learn we were not really listening to the game live and in real time. The technology and budgets did not exist at the time for radio stations to follow teams around the South. Instead, they picked up the games on telegraph and re-created them locally using sound effects that sounded, at least to our young ears, very real. For example, the telegraph would give only very brief details of what was happening and the rest was up to the local announcer sitting inside the station to use his imagination and the sound effects to make it sound like he was at the game. He used the sound of a bat hitting the ball, the sound of a crowd roaring after a good hit or a good play. He ad-libbed about runners playing off base, about pitchers winding up and foul balls back into the stands until he received the next bit of real information on the telegraph. His play-by-play was actually a good bit behind the real action but we never knew the difference. The pseudo radio broadcasts made us believe we were practically at the game in such far-away cities as Birmingham, Atlanta, Nashville, New Orleans and Little Rock. This knowledge put me ahead of my dullard friends at school when our teacher asked where certain cities were located. If the Barons played there, I knew exactly what state it was in. Frankly, it was a real disappointment to learn we were being duped by the technology of the time. Thankfully, I did not know this until I was an adult and, by that time in my life, being duped was sort of par for the course.

The boys in East Florence generally played baseball at the field on Huntsville Road across from the Baptist Church. Over the years that grand field has somehow shrunk into a piece of ground not nearly as big as it is in my memory. It had a backstop and we manufactured the bases out of anything we could find. Our baseball was an old ball without a real cover but we used black tape to keep the string from unwinding. Apparently black electricians tape is not manufactured to withstand being swatted with a bat and bouncing along the ground. The tape soon began to tear apart and would look pretty ragged until one of us raided our father's workshop for a roll of tape and gave the ball a new lease on life. We were re-cycling and didn't even know it. Believe me, a ball that looks like a black flying octopus takes a lot of joy out of the game. Of course, anything that looked like a real ball was better than the rolled up socks we played with in the yard at home.

We also had two or three old wooden bats we carried around with us as we searched for a place to play. Like the ball, the bats were thick with black tape in an attempt to make them usable after being broken. After several tapings, the gummy residue from the tape made a resin bag unnecessary. However, such a purchase would have been extremely unlikely. It was common knowledge that the wooden bat, we didn't know anything about aluminum bats, had to be held in such a position that the trademark was turned up, toward the sky. Otherwise, the bat was easily broken. The intelligence of our ragged team could probably be determined by the amount of tape on our bats. I once received a brand new Louisville Slugger for Christmas with Richie Ashburn's signature. I treated it like the Hope Diamond until some knucklehead turned the trademark the wrong way. Sadly, Richie's bold signature was soon obliterated by black tape.

During the 1950's, my hometown had a semi-pro team called the Florence Raiders. We were blessed because one of our neighbors, Dusty Rickard, had some sort of connection with the team and the old fairgrounds where they played their home games. Our father and Dusty were good friends and we attended many of the Raider's games, probably on free passes because Daddy would never have spent money in such a cavalier manner. Daddy always sat directly behind home plate and spent most of his time yelling at the umpire. We were able to enjoy at least part of the American tradition by going out to the ball park but Daddy couldn't be talked into the peanuts and Cracker Jacks. This association was also profitable for my brother and me because after a Saturday night game, Dusty would take us, along with his son, out to the ball park on Sunday morning to pick up trash. We were paid the princely sum of one dollar in cold hard cash for a job we would have gladly done free of charge. We were also tasked with scouring the area for errant foul balls which had not been found during the game. Occasionally, he would give us an old ball which was long past its prime and could no longer be used. The fact that it was water-logged from lying out in the weather for many weeks was inconsequential. Those old baseballs were heavy and had the consistency of a bowling ball but at least they had a real cowhide cover. The original leather cover was only temporary because a baseball which wound up in our hands had reached the lowest point of its downward spiral and was destined to eventually be covered with black tape.

Most of the kids on our team attended Brandon School but a few of the older guys had somehow managed to be promoted to the junior high school which was located downtown. In just a few years I had to take this same journey from the friendly confines of Brandon to the scary junior high. Ironically, my first teaching job out of college was as a science teacher at this very school. The teachers who were once so intimidating to me were now my colleagues. How had they managed to live so long? Apparently the quiet, skinny kid in the back of the room did not make a lasting impression on them for I was never recognized as a former student. After a few years on the job I was elected to represent them as the leader of their local teachers association. I always feared impeachment was just around the corner if my East Florence roots were ever revealed.

The forced migration into the seventh grade took my older teammates out of the confines of East Florence and gave them an opportunity to mingle with other boys from what we considered to be the affluent parts of town. It wasn't long before they had managed to arrange a pickup game with some of these guys. Since East Florence was considered to be a rather rough neighborhood on the other side of the tracks, they naturally wanted the game to be played elsewhere. The only alternative was a large field called Monumental Park which was a little south of downtown but not in East Florence proper. Those born in the depths of East Florence had specific opinions as to the boundaries of their community. We considered the area called Weeden Heights on the high ground to the east and Catholic Hill to the west to be outside our home territory. Certainly, anything downtown or in the north Florence area required a visa to enter.

The field at Monumental Park was large in comparison to anything we had ever encountered on our home turf. It had a large backstop and a dirt infield practically free of rocks. This is a perk probably not fully appreciated by those who have never played on a field which seemed to produce its own rocks. It is a well-known fact that all the rocks can never be removed from a baseball field. Furthermore, a baseball will seek out any remaining rocks and use them as an excuse to make a bad hop which will inevitably strike a very sensitive part of the body.

We trudged up the hill out of our little community dragging what little equipment we could muster in an old military duffel bag. Our opponent for the day arrived in three station wagons with bags full of equipment, including a mask, chest protector and shin guards for their catcher. It would be a wonderful thing to be able to say we won the game and sent them running back home with their tail between their legs. That type ending generally only happens in Hollywood movies and fairy tales. They actually beat us like a drum. After a brutal defeat we headed back down the hill toward home as they piled back into their wood-grained station wagons on their way out to Howard Johnson's for their choice of twenty-eight flavors of ice cream. In our defense these boys were much better than we were and most played Little League ball. Organized ball was something I had heard about but had no idea how to get involved. This was soon to change.

During my next year at Brandon an announcement was made that any boy between the ages of ten and twelve could try out for one of the Little League teams in Florence. The city recreation department sponsored four National League teams and four American League teams. These eight teams comprised the only organized baseball available to all the boys in the entire city of Florence. Providing an equal opportunity for girls to engage in sports was an idea whose time had not yet come. At that time, only twelve boys were allowed on each team. There were no rules which dictated that every boy had to play in each game. There were no trophies handed out in mass and no team mothers to hand out treats after practice and games. Certainly, there were no team parties. These teams practiced during the week, after school, and played on Saturday at the field in the river bottom, now called McFarland Park. Several of my friends and I decided to try out. Much to our surprise some of us actually made the cut. I was made a member of the Giants, a National League team. Each afternoon after school, we walked down the hill from Brandon and followed the railroad track to the river. There we left the track and walked the short distance to the field. For the first time in my young life I played on a real field with real bases and a pitcher's mound. The field had real dugouts, chalk-lined batter's box and base paths. I wore a real uniform complete with cleats and leggings and there were actually umpires at every game. In my mind it was a miniature Yankee Stadium.

The Little League program was under the direction of Press Robbins who sat in the elevated box above home plate and barked out criticism for bone-headed plays and praise for good plays and good effort. Coach Robbins was not concerned with our self-esteem. Instead, he was attempting to teach us the game of baseball and a few other things which we didn't realize until much later in life. As far as can be determined none of us suffered a damaged psyche and most of us turned out almost normal. He was a man who did not tolerate foolishness from the coaches, the players or their parents. A player or parent who dared question a call by the umpire or acted up in any way was in for a severe public tongue lashing. The world could use more men like Press Robbins to teach young boys the lost art of paying attention and showing respect. Coach Robbins is a legend today among the scores of men who played as boys in the program over the many years he was in charge.

Every boy who has ever played Little League has probably dreamed of playing in the Little League World Series held each year in Pennsylvania. As a twelve year old I was miraculously chosen to represent the Florence Nationals at the District All Star game in Decatur, a nearby city. We practiced for this exciting event for several weeks and journeyed to Decatur with every intention of eventually making it to the World Series. Unfortunately, we were stopped short in our first game by a very large hard-throwing twelve year old kid who threw fastballs that looked like a baby aspirin as it streaked to the plate. Not all dreams come to fruition and ours went up in smoke. But in my case, I felt fortunate just to be along for the ride.

As a reward for making the All Star team Daddy took me and my brother to Birmingham to watch our beloved Barons play the Memphis Chicks. We caught a Greyhound bus in downtown Florence which took us to the huge station in downtown Birmingham. From there we took our first taxi ride out to the now historic Rickwood Field for the game where we were able to see with our own eyes our hero, Johnny Blanchard. We returned home by bus late that night. It was quite a day for two youngsters who had rarely left East Florence.

It saddens me to see the state of major league baseball today. The prevalence of drugs, high salaries and the gross commercialization has turned the game into something hard to attract any interest. The Little League World Series in Williamsport, Pennsylvania, is something I try to watch every year. Dreams may die an early death but their memory lingers on and never entirely disappears. The Yankees are so far from the brick wall in my old yard they may as well be playing on Venus.

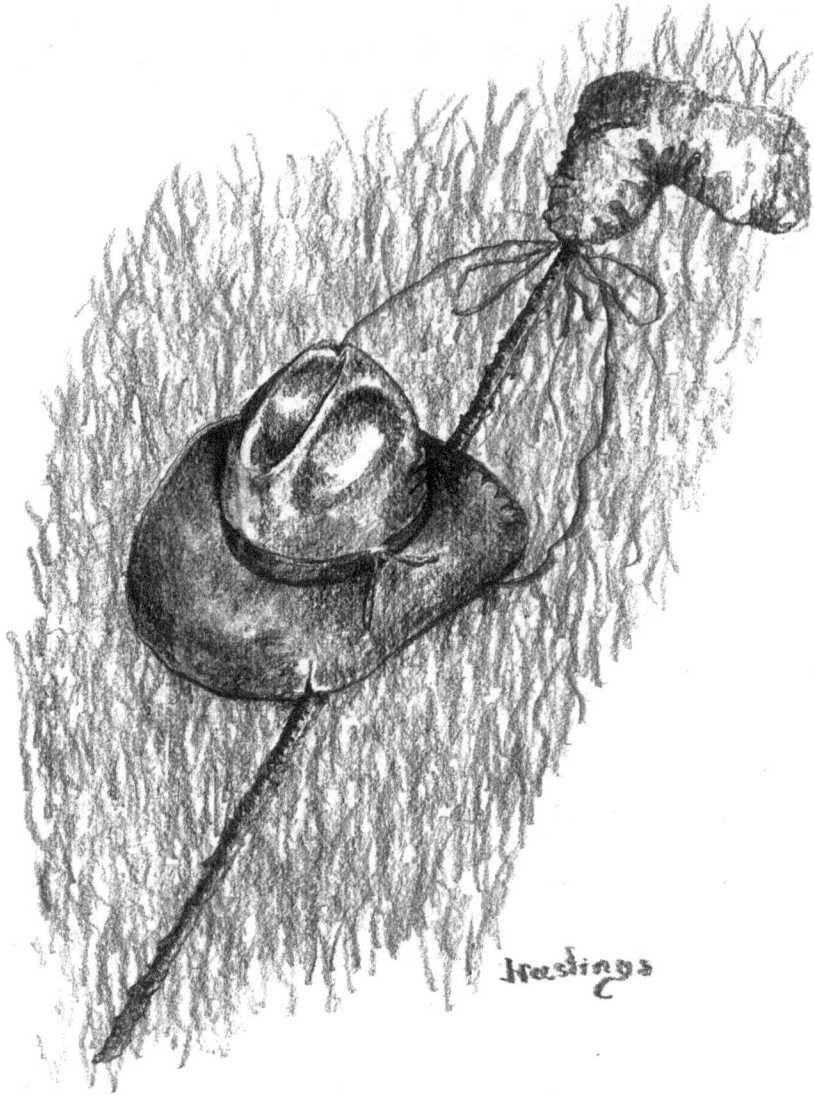

Heroes and Cowboys

Heroes seem to be sort of hard to come by in today's world. In my own case, when I scan the ranks of those who normally come to mind and are generally associated with a place on the proverbial pedestal, I look up and discover the pedestal is empty. Growing older has taught me many things and one of the most important is that being perfect is a trait humans will never attain. Our longevity on this planet has done little, or nothing, for us as a species to learn from the mistakes of others. Sometimes I believe we take two steps forward and three steps back. Of course, perfection is not what we are seeking here, only a few positive traits which we can admire.

There are a lot of things kids growing up today have to face that my generation never had to even consider. Much has been said and written about the topic and being even more redundant is not my intention. That being said, probably the saddest difference is the absolute failure of many of the people who normally would be on a kid's list of heroes to try to live up to even the lowest of standards. The behavior some of these folks display in public is so out of touch with the way most of us think we should live is beyond comprehension. In other words, where have all the heroes gone? Far be it from me to try and fathom what goes through the mind of today's young folks but I can't begin to figure out the reasoning behind some of people they admire and even adore. The scoundrels they choose at the top of their list would have been tarred and feathered and run out of town on a rail when I was growing up in the 1950's and 60's.

One possible explanation is that they have very little from which to choose. Have we, as a society, lost all perspective when it comes to setting standards of conduct anything like what we were taught as children? At times, I believe the bar has been set so low a snake would have a hard time slithering under it. Please believe me when I say I am definitely not comparing some of today's celebrities to snakes. This comparison would be an insult to the snakes.

To my antiquated way of thinking, one of the chief reasons things are so different is the means of communication open to today's young people as compared to what was available to kids of the 1950s. All of us had the old standby, word of mouth. A few people had telephones when I was a boy and radios were generally found in most homes. Of course, being on a party line spread gossip like wildfire around a community about as well as anything. One old fellow in the community had a wife named Wanda. He was fond of saying that the fastest method of spreading news was the telegraph, the telephone and tell-a-Wanda. However, even that had its limits and the prattle generally died out when it began to reach uninterested ears. At our old house, a television finally came along toward the late 1950's. My mother lamented for years because all the kids in the neighborhood seemed to gravitate toward her house. That was true because she had so many kids there was always something going on and someone always willing to come outside and play. After we managed to get a television, adults began hanging around, particularly on Saturday night when wrestling was the hottest commodity in the old neighborhood. It was understandable why the phrase, "going viral," was not yet a part of our world.

But, there are gizmos available today that can zip information around the world at the speed of light. Vast amounts of very important information are conveyed almost instantly from continent to continent, from capital to capital, from screen to screen and to the eyes of young folks. This remarkable advancement has certainly made all of our lives different, some in good ways and some in not so good ways. Consequently, the same amount of not so important information, my mother would have called it "trash", can also be moved in a flash and that has been somewhat of a problem with young minds unable to sort out the good from the bad. At the end of the day, many adults have the same problem. These devices come on the market so fast that yesterday's hot item is obsolete tomorrow. When computers were coming into their heyday it was said when you bought a new computer you should just go ahead and toss it into the trash on your way out of the store because it was already obsolete. That is now true with all the telephones which seem to appear about every other month. Slick advertising labels each new one as "the next generation." Mob scenes are common at retail outlets as a gullible public scrambles, "to keep up with the Jones." In our old neighborhood, even the Jones couldn't afford one of those gizmos.

To those of us whose hair has turned gray, a computer the size of a pickup truck is still a miracle to behold. Of course, it doesn't take much to be an improvement over the two tin cans connected by a long string we played with as kids. Those of us in the baby boomer generation consider it a marvelous achievement to be able to master one of these wonders of the world to the point it can be put to practical use. Our problem is that many of us continue to use computers the size of a truck while the rest of the world has graduated to a computerized phone half the size of a Prince Albert can. These phones can be used for so many things they can be downright scary. It is a great comfort to have a phone in my pocket to use if needed. It sure beats the heck out of searching for a pay phone in the middle of the night. The mere fact I would refer to something as obsolete as a pay phone reveals a lot about my standing in the world of technology. However, my children claim my phone isn't any good if I never turn it on. Maybe I don't turn it on for a good reason.

The generation gap rears its ugly head again because today's kids consider anything with wires attached is something only a caveman, or their grandparents, would own. For people like me, having a wire attached to an electronic device is the equivalent of a security blanket. Folks in my age group tend to have a better understanding of devices which not only have wires but also possess moving parts they can see actually functioning. An electric can opener comes immediately to mind. What a marvelous device! A better example might be something like an old-time cash register. These things must have had a thousand inter-meshing moving parts. It was sort of understandable because it depended upon using levers, cogs and wheels to make it function. In other words, the parts were visible. They were something we could see and touch. By removing the outer shell one could easily visualize that if you pressed a key, it was connected by levers and springs to other parts and eventually, if it was kept oiled and clean, the desired action would take place. These old machines, unlike computers, did not hurl gigabytes, or whatever, thousands of miles into the stratosphere and bounce them off a satellite orbiting our planet and then somehow mysteriously return to earth and locate the machine it was sent to find only a few seconds earlier. So many bewildering things happen when I press the "send" button on my cell phone I get a headache just thinking about it. Maybe the bottom line is that if a little WD-40, a screwdriver and some duct tape can't fix it then it is beyond our understanding, kind of like an Ouija board.

Folks seeking attention know full well the power of publicity, good or bad. As a matter of fact, many times negative attention serves their purpose much better than positive. Their livelihood depends upon staying in the public eye and they have become expert at doing so. These individuals have also figured out that any deed, or misdeed, they might choose to engage in will be on the tiny screens of literally millions of people all over the world in a matter of minutes, if not nanoseconds, whatever that is. World-wide instant publicity is now virtually free due to technology. Much of the global panic and outrage we see today could be avoided if we reverted to sending the news by letter. Events would have calmed down considerably by the time the mail arrived.

In the field of entertainment, there are many folks with so little talent they are forced to use language that wouldn't even be appropriate for a bunch of drunken sailors in a bar room brawl. They know full well that by using foul and vile words, they will receive attention worldwide and it will all be free. Consequently, young folks constantly hear and see the names of these individuals on their tiny little gizmos and they wind up being

65

admired for all the wrong reasons. It makes me wonder how in the world entertainers of my youth like Red Skelton, Bob Hope, Jack Benny, Jonathan Winters, Lucille Ball, Carol Burnett, Tim Conway and many others managed to make a living. They made millions laugh because they were talented and truly funny. They practiced their craft for years and honed their talent with hard work and were able to earn their place in the hearts of generations of Americans. They did not have to resort to the antics of the generation of foul mouth individuals of today who try to pass themselves off as entertainers.

The world was replete with individuals to admire when I was a kid. In my world, however, it was mostly athletes and cowboys. Maybe it was really movie stars impersonating cowboys but I didn't know the difference. However, all of them had one thing in common: they had actually done something worthwhile to warrant being adored by their young fans. We were mercifully uninformed of their private lives and that is the way it should be. The chief difference was the way they conducted themselves in public and most were careful to keep their public lives very respectable. If they somehow ran afoul of the public trust there was no way to tattle to the rest of the world within seconds. Facebook and Tweets were years down the road. They weren't surrounded by adoring fans equipped with a camera phone.

Some of my heroes were baseball players, others were Olympic athletes, racing jockeys, college athletes or coaches and maybe a few horses and dogs thrown in to add a little variety. Some of the people considered celebrities today have achieved absolutely nothing worthy of being admired by anyone, except maybe their mother. Unfortunately, as a school counselor I found that most mothers are extremely poor judges of their child's character. Even mass murderers are defended by their mother. Many of today's so-called celebrities are, as someone else put it, famous for being famous. Is our world so depleted of people to admire we are now resorting to conveying hero status on many who simply do not deserve it? Unfortunately, I believe the answer is a resounding yes!

Most of my heroes rode horses, or were horses that let people ride them. I grew up riding the range with Roy and Trigger, the Lone Ranger and Silver, Tonto and Scout, Gene and Champ, the Cisco Kid and Diablo, Marshal Dillon and Buck, Hopalong Cassidy and Topper, Zorro and Tornado, Hoss and Chub, Little Joe and Cochise, and Lash Larue and Black Diamond, just to name a few. And, yes, to prove I am not a sexist pig, Dale Evans and Buttermilk. While lying on the living room floor in our old house listening to the giant radio, the thrill of the opening notes of the show's signature and highly recognizable background music, the *William Tell Overture,* sent chills coursing up and down my young spine. On a daily basis, around supper time, this classical music summoned the Lone

Ranger, and his huge white horse Silver, to come-a-running because injustice had once again appeared on the scene and needed his immediate attention. The Ranger, along with his trusted sidekick Tonto, ferreted out the bad guys and restored peace and tranquility to a town almost quicker than he could utter the famous words, "Hi-yo Silver, away," and then gallop off into the sunset searching for more bad guys.

This enchantment with riders and their horse carried well over into my high school years. My tenth grade world history teacher, Mr. Lindsey Allen, spent considerable time on some fellow by the name of Alexander the Great and I paid absolutely no attention until he happened to mention he had a famous horse, Bucephalus. It is amazing what will grab the attention of kids, even teenagers. According to historical legend, this horse was virtually untouchable by everyone who approached it, except the young teen-ager, Alexander. It makes sense to figure his title, "The Great," only came along after he actually conquered the known world and accomplished something worthy of the handle. The fact that Mr. Allen even knew the name of a horse elevated him considerably in my estimation. It is also interesting that this very horse was the inspiration for one of the greatest series of books young horse lovers have ever known. The **Black Stallion** books featured a huge black stallion which could only be ridden by his young master, Alec Ramsay. Find me a horse-loving kid who has not read and been thrilled by these books and I will show you a kid raised in a cave by goats.

My heroes and their horses mentioned above became known to me by a variety of methods other than reading. There was one blossoming creation which made Saturday morning a day which was eagerly anticipated by thousands of young folks across the country: the Saturday morning movie matinee. The old Princess theatre on Tennessee Street in Florence was the site of these marvelous movies for my generation. This was long before the time of mega-theatres where a customer has the choice of eight movies in the same building. There was one building, one screen and no option. We walked, rode our bikes and somehow made our way downtown from all parts of town and the county. Each Saturday morning, for the admittance price of one thin dime, kids flocked to the picture show, as we called it, to see what came to be called cliff-hangers. They were literally the only show in town as most of us did not have the luxury of a television at home. For the dime, we were treated to a cartoon, a newsreel, coming attractions and the main attraction. The newsreels were intended to give the audience the top news items of the week but generally had the effect of convincing most of us the Russians were going to blow us all to smithereens. Bomb shelters sprang up all over the country as a result of these newsreels. Maybe if all the bad news of today came to us by a newsreel seen only at the movies, the stock market wouldn't go into a death spiral so often, sometimes without any apparent reason at all. Cleverly, the movies always picked up on last week's episode which inevitably left the hero in a very dire predicament, or hanging from a cliff, so-to-speak. These things went on forever and resulted in a generation of addicted kids living on the edge until we plopped down our dime the next Saturday. It was always necessary to return the next week to find out what happened. Of course, I have never watched any of today's soap operas on television but I hear they are laid out in much the same format. In hindsight, I am really glad Saturday was the day the theatres featured these movies. My mother was fully convinced that to attend a picture show on Sunday was a mortal sin and was not shy about making known the destination of my soul if temptation got the best of me.

In those old movies, the hero always won and very few people died in the process. There was no blood and gore, no complicated plots, and absolutely no steamy sex scenes. I don't recall Roy or the Ranger ever being anything but gallant around females and children. The heroes always stood up for the oppressed little guy and good always won out over evil. Thieves and outlaws were frequently subdued by firing as many as twenty rounds from a six shooter without the hindrance of having to re-load. Watching some re-runs of the Roy Rogers movies has convinced me that Roy had more fist fights than any man alive. The miraculous thing about these fights was that he never lost any teeth, suffered a bloody nose or a serious concussion from all the blows to his head. Somehow, Roy managed to escape from a fight without even the appearance of being ruffled and banged-up. The only way Roy or the Ranger ever lost a fight was to be accosted by a whole gang of thugs or clubbed over the head from behind by the long barrel of a six-shooter. The bad guys were called by such unsavory names as hombre, owl-hoot, crook, scoundrel and rascal. They were easily recognized as villains and it was not unusual for the audience to break out into a full-throated cheer when our hero's heroic action brought about their demise. The very worst four-letter word might be "dang." None of the filthy, not fit for human ears kind of conversations common today in movies, and even piped into our homes on television, was ever heard in these innocent settings. Unlike us, today's youth can master an obscene vocabulary simply by watching television without the benefit of older brothers and graffiti on restroom walls. Justice always prevailed and the good guy never failed to win the girl, if one was around. Inevitably, the presence of a female would distract from the non-stop action and was extremely annoying to most of us. When our hero grew lonely, he would just pick up his guitar and sing around the campfire, somehow accompanied by what sounded like a choral ensemble totally unseen by the naïve viewers. My personal preference would have been to leave out all the singing and get on with the shooting but if Roy wanted to sing, let him sing. Incredibly, at the end of each show, the Lone Ranger and Tonto simply rode off into the sunset in search of more injustice to stamp out. These two idols were the exact opposite of the characters which slime and slither their way across the media outlets of today. They actually shunned the spotlight and were satisfied with the fact that once again good and honorable men had won out over the bad guys. As immature as all this sounds to today's sophisticated masses, it did have a positive impression on generations of young people. Even though we didn't always show it, we did know right from wrong.

Comic books were also the source of much of the hero culture of the 1950's. These little literary treasures could be purchased for ten cents and were probably responsible for millions of kids finding something of interest to help them learn to read. One does not have to read the classics to improve as a reader. Horrors, I hope English teachers are not reading this nonsense. My dad made me a large wooden box in which I kept my most valuable possessions. It was filled to the brim with comic books of my cowboy heroes but also super heroes such as Superman, Batman, Rubber Man, Iron Man and Aqua Man. My best friend and cousin, Mike, also had a stash of comic books. We traded them like Wall Street brokers trade pork bellies and grain futures. To my way of thinking, reading most anything which interests a person will help improve reading skills: even if it happens to be on a box of cereal. As with many of my opinions, this is contrary to what most knowledgeable professionals believe to be true.

However, there was a side to our entertainment which was not really concerned with the nobility of mankind. It was reflected in the popularity of such literature as the notorious, **Mad** magazine. In the early 1950's, this irreverent comic book became a monthly magazine. Maybe the best way to describe it would be to call it a printed version of the popular television show of today, **Saturday Night Live.** The magazine featured a dullard in residence named Alfred E. Newman who became an iconic figure to those of us with a twisted sense of humor. The sole purpose of the magazine was to poke fun at anything and everything: nothing was excluded. This darker side to our interest was reflected on the silver screen in the form of the **Three Stooges**, which did not speak well for the future of this nation. Fortunately, our parents were not well informed about the foolish and nonsensical behavior of this trio or the movie theatre would have been deemed off limits and a bad influence on our budding character development. The Stooges were the stars of countless low-budget, generally short movies which made virtually no sense but were hilariously funny, at least to some of us. Much to my dismay and surprise, I have actually run across individuals who do not like, or even appreciate, the comedy of the Stooges. If those zany characters could not make you laugh maybe a sense of humor transplant might be in order.

The world has travelled far from the absolute right and wrong values most of us were taught as children. Political correctness has made the values many of us believe made this country something unique virtually a thing of the past. To see how far we have strayed we only have to look at a few examples of behavior which is deemed acceptable today. It is not unusual to hear of birth control devices being distributed in junior high school. It is virtually a crime for parents to discipline their children. Doctors are forbidden to tell parents their daughter has come in for an abortion. Our schools have armed guards while teachers in some areas are actually permitted to bring weapons to protect themselves. Nativity scenes have been banned by some cities as a result of one or two people complaining. Prayers are banned before public events and at school. The cross which has for centuries been symbolic of a belief in God has been attacked in every manner possible and removed from areas where they have stood for many years. Marijuana is legally sold in stores in some states. The bottom line is that behavior which was once considered wrong, and probably deviant, is now celebrated by many in the public eye.

The world of my youth was far from perfect and probably had many more fly specks on the wall than I remember. But it was certainly a much simpler and in many ways kinder world than the one we live in now. Some changes are good and we have undergone a multitude of changes as a society which have made the world better in a lot of ways. On the other hand, the loss of a generation of heroes truly worth our admiration has caused many young folks to lose sight of what is good and focus on things that are not so good. Our nation has suffered as a result of this change.

One of the truly great baseball legends of my early years was Joe DiMaggio who played centerfield for the New York Yankees during the 1950' and 60's. He was called "Joltin Joe" because of his uncanny ability to hit a baseball. Joe DiMaggio was universally known as a decent man. Of course, we don't know anything about his personal life but that is the point. He lived his public life in a way which earned the respect of people all over the world. A popular duo known as Simon and Garfunkel recorded a song during the 1960's which lamented the loss of so many American values and ideals. This song went by the title, "Mrs. Robinson." There is a line in this song which goes to the heart of what I am trying to say.

"Where have you gone Joe DiMaggio
Our nation turned its lonely eyes to you.
What's that you say, Mrs. Robinson,
Joltin Joe has left and gone away."

"Joltin Joe" has indeed left and gone away, along with a whole host of other heroes worthy of the admiring eyes of a nation. Will they ever return or will generations of Americans aimlessly grasp at straw figures? Young folks may have a good reason to be confused.

High School in the 60's

The girl of my dreams sat just literally inches from me. Unfortunately, we were separated by a thick piece of steel, namely in the form of the thick metal floor of a 1955 DeSoto. Things frequently do not work out the way a sixteen year boy intended and this was definitely one of those times. You see, we were only inches apart, but I was underneath the car and she was sitting primly, I suppose, in the passenger seat awaiting my return. Underneath the old car, I was desperately attempting to maneuver the stiff piece of bailing wire through what was left of the old rusted hanger from which the muffler and tailpipe once were suspended. During my former life as a teenager, the most trusted tool in my rather limited arsenal was bailing wire. Did I mention I was lying in about two inches of water? We were on our very first date, cruising down Court Street, when the muffler and tailpipe suddenly fell off the car and we were engulfed in a loud roaring noise which drowned out any possibility of a conversation. This might have been a good thing because I had no idea what to say to her. Most teenage boys are not good conversationalists and I was certainly no exception.

A prudent question might be why didn't I just continue on down the street and act like I had a loud, fast, souped-up car like most of the other young dudes? For one thing, it is impossible to make a 1955 DeSoto look, or sound, like anything other than what it really is, a 1955 DeSoto. My dad's car was just one in a long line of used vehicles with several things in common. All were huge, heavy and cumbersome. Did I mention ugly? Another thing the owners had in common was relief that gasoline could be purchased for about twenty-five cents per gallon. It was my belief that DeSotos were really reincarnations of Sherman tanks left-over from World War II, which ended about the time I was born. The cars weighed about the same as the tanks but had been re-shaped and emerged from the assembly line as a family sedan with all the other characteristics of the tank. Because of their weight and bulk the car body was very low to the ground. Many of the old dirt roads had well-worn ruts which were apparently permanent features. It was rumored some folks were forced to drive around for hours in a vain effort to free their tires from the iron grip of the deep ruts. When they froze during the winter it was like steel on steel when the car bottom contacted the frozen mud. A low slung car could easily loose something off the under carriage when the wheels dropped into one of these deep ruts. Unfortunately, a few weeks earlier the muffler on the DeSoto became the victim of one of these ruts and I had wired it back into place and had not yet had the time to tell Daddy. The fact that bailing wire was not a permanent fix was the main reason for my predicament. Lying underneath the car in a puddle of water with my date seated above

73

my head wondering what was going on could have been a form of payback from God for my procrastination.

There was an urgency to put the exhaust system back into place because of the distinct chance I would be returning to the Florence city jail if I had failed to do so. I was driving my daddy's car because my 1955 Chevrolet, also minus a muffler and tailpipe, had apparently irritated one of Florence's finest about a week prior to this particular night. It was on a Saturday night, much like this one except it was not raining. A few friends and I were cruising Court Street, which was the main thing to do back then. Apparently every teenager in Lauderdale, Colbert and a few other counties wasted time and gas every weekend by repeatedly cruising Court Street. The routine was to turn around on north Court in front of Rogers Hall and slowly drive back south. The southern terminus was left to the individual's discretion. Why this was necessary remains a mystery to me to this very day.

At the north end of the street sat a police cruiser watching this strange ritual play out and fervently hoping some scofflaw, like me, would do something to relieve the boredom of a long night on patrol. The fact some of my heathen friends were leaning out the back windows making obscene hand gestures to the other cars did not help matters. My car, with no muffler, would have attracted attention even in the middle of a kamikaze attack. There was no way we were going to escape their full scrutiny under the circumstances. All these factors combined obviously violated some kind of obscure city ordinance so I was pulled over. One of the officers emerged from the cruiser and swaggered to my car. When he bent down to look in the window, I became suddenly alarmed because I recognized him immediately. It seemed a onetime nemesis of some of my older brothers back when we lived in East Florence was about to bring his boring Saturday night to an end by having some fun at my expense. He had somehow become a police officer and I had given him a golden opportunity to extract some skin from one of the McDonald clan.

The story told in our family was that one of my brothers had once given him quite a thrashing when they were younger and resulted in some bad feelings between the two families. Does the Bible mention that the sins of the older brothers frequently come to rest on the shoulders of the youngest brother? If not, maybe it should. My identity was confirmed when he looked at my license. He began smiling like a cat playing with a doomed mouse. No further identification was needed because he immediately told me to get out of my car and into the back seat of the police cruiser. Much to the amusement of my friends, he drove away and left them sitting on Court Street in my car. The view from

74

the back seat of a police car did not provide the same amount of satisfaction I was experiencing earlier with my friends while cruising the exact same street. Maintaining any semblance of dignity is difficult under these circumstances. While it was not exactly a walk to the gallows, I knew it would not turn out well for me. I must say I was not water-boarded or beaten with a night stick but I was taken to the interrogation room and questioned extensively about my lack of knowledge concerning what they considered to be moving traffic violations. Thankfully, there was no loud noise ordinance at the time. For some reason, they kept repeating something about reckless driving and speeding. Heck, I thought it was just the muffler. After about thirty minutes of watching me sweat bullets, they agreed to overlook the speeding and reckless driving in exchange for my promise to fix the muffler. This was my first experience with what is now known as a plea bargain. In addition I had to agree to tell my daddy about my trip to the police station: if not, they would. Why didn't they just shoot me? After their fun for the night was over, they graciously provided me a free ride back to my car to suffer another barrage of questions from my idiot friends. A good case could be made that they were, at the very least, partly responsible for my predicament.

So, I was sort of between the proverbial rock and hard place. The reason I had asked Daddy to use his car in the first place was that I could not chance meeting up with officer friendly again on my big date and caught driving the same car without a muffler after I had promised to fix it. There was no established time table on the repair and I fully intended to keep my word. Now I was in danger of being pulled over again for driving a different car with the same problem. Another new phrase for my expanding vocabulary was "repeat offender."

Even my feeble teenage brain knew it would not be a good first impression to arrive at my date's house driving what appeared to be a reject from the demolition derby. My initial attempt at a good first impression had failed miserably a few days earlier when I had called her house to ask her out. Her mother answered the phone, and in my zeal to secure a date before losing my nerve, I thought I was talking to the daughter. When asked if she would go to the movie with me she said she would love to but first would have to ask her husband. My already jangled nerves caused my tongue to make strange noises and I was just about to hang up the phone when she mercifully informed me maybe I was calling for her daughter. Her howls of laughter could easily be heard as she summoned my date-to-be to the phone. Strike one!

After knocking on the front door the father had asked me some very serious and probing questions about my background. It was highly possible his wife had told him about the phone call and he needed some assurance I was not mentally deranged. He seemed to be having a lot of doubt as to whether or not I could be trusted to take proper care of his daughter. The sight of the old DeSoto out front seemed to mollify him somewhat and he finally left the room. I took his departure as permission for her to leave with me.

However, I was quite certain that if I had not been able to replace the muffler and tail pipe on the DeSoto, my fate was sealed because there was no way I could escape another trip to the lockup when caught for the same offense for the second time in two weeks. On our previous trip down the street I had spotted my friend on the police force sitting in the exact same spot as before. He smiled and waved as we passed so he knew who was behind the wheel of the DeSoto. If the unthinkable happened, my date's father would never appreciate the fact I was a victim of police harassment. His chief concern would be how in the world I considered leaving her in the car alone while I was carted off by the police to even come close to my vow to take care of his little princess. Permission for a second date would be out of the question.

My desperate efforts underneath the car succeeded but it had already rained on my parade, literally and figuratively. As promised, she was delivered to her front door before the prescribed curfew. At school the next Monday, she did say her father was curious why water was dripping from my clothes when I left her at the front door. The scoundrel was obviously peeping out the window. This was a definite sign of a lack of trust. Strike two!

After a couple more dates it became quite obvious this romance was never going to get off the ground. The final indignity took place when she sent one of my friends to my house to tell me not to call her again. Since we were not actually going together, there was no need for her to observe the protocol of a formal break-up. Surely, after all I had been through, I deserved at least a phone call or a hand-written note. Much later in life, I learned that God does not answer our prayers the way we think we want them answered. Strike three!

The sad scenario described above was unfortunately the story of many teenage boys when confronted with the terror associated with asking a girl out on a date. For some reason, I believe that same level of stress does not exist with many of today's young people. They can communicate in so many ways using technology that surely good and bad vibes can be picked up without having to make an absolute fool of oneself.

In my day, about the only place available to pick up vibes, other than school, was the old skating rink in Spring Park. However, none of us were remotely aware of anything called vibes at the time. The guys who owned their own pair of shoe skates seemed to be very popular with the girls and obviously had a monopoly on the vibes. Most of them wore black leather jackets with their hair slicked back and had a pack of Lucky Strike cigarettes rolled into the sleeve of their white tee shirt. These same guys wore shoes equipped with metal heel taps and drove fast cars which later became classics. To my knowledge, none of them drove a 1955 Desoto. They could skate backwards and do some serious twisting and turning maneuvers at high speed. It was highly likely my skating technique featuring a rather awkward flailing of both arms and running into the rail in order to come to a stop made me something less than impressive. However, the fact that I skated dozens of times with rented skates without breaking a bone or coming down with foot rash was quite an achievement.

The one thing I remember fondly about the skating rink was the very cool music they played as the skaters whizzed around the ring. The music of the late 1950's and all through the 1960's had to be among the best of all time. We skated to the sound of Roy Orbison, The Big Bopper, Ricky Nelson, Conway Twitty, Connie Francis and so many others. If we ever were fortunate enough to own a car with a radio we listened to such greats as Peter, Paul, and Mary, the Mommas and Poppas, the Kingston Trio, the Lovin' Spoonfuls, the Beach Boys, Chubby Checker, and the Monkees. We were treated to classic lyrics like the one with the line, "A-Wop-Bop-A-Loo-Mop-A-Bop-Bam-Boom." Others include the deep and meaningful line, "Do-Wah-Diddy-Diddy-Dum-Diddy-Do" and the immortal, "Sha-La-La-La-La-La-La-La." Adults considered the strange language used in these songs to be a sure sign of a decadent generation.

Like young folks everywhere, we ignored what the adults were thinking and sang along as if we knew exactly what they meant. And how many tears were shed, boys and girls alike, when Floyd Kramer's classical instrumental on the piano, *Last Date*, was played over the radio? Memories of unrequited love were more than most of us could bear. It would have made me cry if I had any memories of a last date but old Floyd Kramer could have been a tractor mechanic for all I knew. My theme song would have been something like, *The One and Only Date*, but, sadly, it never made the charts.

A date for most teenagers during that stage of our life consisted mostly of a movie and then capping off the night by going to a burger joint. The old Princess, Norwood, Colbert and Majestic theaters are long gone and the Shoals and Ritz have seen many different lives since their heyday as the center of entertainment for many generations of teenagers. One of the truly unique places to take a date would have been one of the two drive-ins in the area. The site of the drive-ins such as the Joy Land and Wilson are virtually unrecognizable in their present state of development. The land on which the former Joy Land sat is now occupied by a giant church whose members may or may not be aware of the thousands of carnal transgressions committed on the property during its former life. It was possible to save the price of admittance to a drive-in by hiding in the trunk. After Margo and I began dating, obviously at my insistence, she was willing to suffer the humiliation of being let out of the trunk after we had conned the ticket taker at the gate. It was highly possible she was clairvoyant and foresaw the lean years ahead after we were married. The greatest deal of all was when the drive-in had a dollar per carload night when every vehicle was crammed to the gills with cheapskates. In my case it was necessary to pinch every penny in order to buy tubes of Clearasil for my terminal case of acne and jars of Butch Wax to keep my flat top in good shape. However one managed to gain admittance, once inside it became sort of a picnic atmosphere. Many people got out their food baskets and spread blankets on the ground to sit and enjoy the movie. Their children played on the swings and the slide until the lights blinked signaling the movie was about to begin. Some of the windows on many cars, usually on the back row alongside the pickup trucks, remained closed and quickly fogged over, indicating those inside were not interested in playing outside. When I smell popcorn popping today, I recall the same smell drifting from the concession stand and into the open car windows. It was easy to spot the folks on their first visit to the drive-in. Many of them drove away with the speaker still attached to their car window. After we were married, Margo and I continued to go to the Joy Land occasionally and actually witnessed one fellow make a complete spectacle of himself on what was obviously his first visit. He parked beside us, got out of his car and walked around the speaker pole, checking it out very carefully. Finally, he turned to the lady in the car, who was undoubtedly his wife and shouted, "Honey, this thing's got concrete poured around it." I am sure his dear wife made absolutely sure this tale was told in their family for generations.

After the movie, we usually migrated to one of the eating places where teenagers of the day gathered. The original Chat-n-Chew in Petersville offered not only food but a free movie on the giant screen of the Joy Land Drive-In located next door. It was not unusual to see people sprawled on the hood of their car or sitting in the bed of a truck watching whatever movie might be playing at the time. The video was great but the audio left something to be desired. It was helpful to be a lip reader. The Frosty King up the road offered the best shakes and coldest drinks to be found anywhere in their frosted glass mugs. The Woody Mac across the bridge was a treat because you were served while seated inside your car. If one wanted to really splurge, the Shanty in downtown Florence offered a hamburger steak and fries that was hard to beat but a crowd of mostly adults had to be tolerated. This was also the case at Sammy's Cellar. There was also a little known place called, The Rendezvous, located on South Court Street almost to O'Neal Bridge. Its location made it difficult to get into and out of the parking lot. They had a giant burger which was so large it was difficult even for a teenage boy to eat. Any girls who could master one of those gigantic burgers would certainly be worth taking home to meet the parents.

There are a lot of good things I remember about high school but there are a few I would truly like to forget and most of that involves serious lapses in my personal behavior. Looking back on my time as a student and on my career in education there are night and day differences between the two. One truly unique thing I do remember is I had a study hall with Mr. Spillers in the Ag building. Almost every day one of his students would bring his hunting rifle or shotgun into class to be admired or to do some kind of repair. Virtually every pickup truck in the parking lot had a gun rack in the rear window on which hung a prized firearm. What other evidence do we need to show that times have changed more than anyone would ever have thought? I remember the break during the day when students were allowed to sit in their cars or trucks or go out to the pines behind the school and smoke. As I recall, there seemed to be a lot of scores settled out in the pines because of the frequency of fights. Maybe it was a case where the fighters went to the pines and the lovers went to the front parking lot. During my career as a high school counselor there was a great deal of time, effort and money expended in keeping students away from the parking lot and away from tobacco of any kind. They were immediately arrested and hauled to jail if they brought anything resembling a firearm or knife to school.

I remember cherry bombs going off in chemistry class and a daily explosion of firecrackers in the trash barrel in the breeze way between the old building and the old gym. This type event certainly detracts from the learning process but we did receive a good education, frequently in spite of ourselves. This is evidenced by the number of Central graduates who have had professional careers in law, the military, medicine, education, politics and business and have had a good life in other areas of employment because of the extraordinary efforts of our teachers in a state where our schools continue to be underfunded to this very day.

One of the similarities between my time as a high school student and my career in education is the number of cliques which seem to flourish among students in a school. Students who have grown up in a school and known their classmates since the first grade have a difficult time understanding what it means to someone new who enters the school from the outside. This is especially true in high school. That atmosphere existed at Central as well as the schools where I worked and at virtually every school in the country even today. As much as I wanted to be accepted in my new school, I failed to realize there were others struggling with the identical problem. I regret not being part of the solution and shudder to think I may have been part of the problem. A circle of people who have been close friends for a long time is almost impossible to break, sort of like the Red Rover game we played as children. The same situation exists outside of a school as well. The human race will have reached a great milestone when we become more concerned about inclusion rather than exclusion.

I remember pep rallies and Friday night football games. I remember finally earning a letter sweater which I wore with more pride than necessary. I remember a Beta Club trip to the convention in Birmingham where I marveled my first taste of a Krystal hamburger. I remember the day the announcement came over the speaker that President Kennedy had been killed. I was sitting in Mrs. Wanda Trollinger's senior English class at the time. Little did we know the politics of our country had been re-directed by an assassin's bullet and thus began the gradual loss of the innocence our nation had enjoyed since its' birth. I remember the pride I felt when I received my class ring and the utter sadness when Margo and I both sold our class rings to a fly-by-night gold dealer set up in a motel room downtown. Paying bills always trumps the desire to hold on to a class ring. Finally, I remember the last day of our senior year and many of us feeling as if we were escaping from prison. It didn't take long for me to realize we were not as smart as we had thought because soon we cherished those years spent at Central High School. It is too bad that most of us do not have the foresight to recognize special moments in real time and treat them as such. By the time we look back and realize their uniqueness, they are gone forever. Graduation night, in late May of 1964, was the last time the entire class was together as a group and the last time many of us would ever see some of our classmates.

The one really significant thing I remember about high school is the unbelievable patience our principal, Mr. Joel Brewer, showed toward me and some of my classmates. He was willing to give me second, third, fourth and fifth chances to begin acting like a human being. If today's zero tolerance policies had been in place during my time in high school I would have never been able to graduate and my life would have been drastically different. Many of us treated this fine man as an adversary when he was really the best friend we had at the time. To his credit, he only chuckles when I offer another apology.

My generation was the first wave of what came to be called the Baby Boomers who came along after the end of World War II. We were born into the aftermath of this war and we were infants when the Korean conflict rolled around. Many of my classmates went into the military immediately after graduation and were caught up in the war in Vietnam.

We lived through all these wars along with the great civil rights struggle of the 1960's with violent protests in cities and on college campuses. Some of the great music of our time was the protest songs of the 1960's. We not only remember when President Kennedy was killed but also his brother Bobby, a presidential candidate at the time. An assassin also took the life of Dr. Martin Luther King in nearby Memphis and four little girls were murdered in a Baptist church on a September Sunday morning in Birmingham. Our nation was rocked by violence and unrest and its citizens seemed to be at war with each other. All the time the wars and killings were taking place, we were in the middle of the Cold War and experienced many drills in school in case we were bombed by the Russians. We now know that crawling under a flimsy desk will not protect a person from a nuclear blast or the resulting fallout, but what else could we do?

Many of the really stupid and zany things teenagers do is because they fear being rejected by their peers. Acceptance by the pack is a driving force with many of God's creatures, not just people. For some strange reason, this caused me to believe that rolling yards would make me a more acceptable and well-rounded person. Much later in life, I found this was not universally true. The father of some of the girls whose yards we rolled did not agree. My wife of almost fifty years had a step-father who used a shotgun to show the level of his disagreement when he caught me and some of my other witless friends merrily decorating the trees in his front yard. At the first blast, we scattered like quail into ditches and barbed wire fences. Fortunately, it was a very dark night and absolute identification was not possible. Yet, he did have his doubts and his suspicions about me were confirmed when I accidentally ran over his beloved dog after leaving Margo at home one night. As ridiculous as it may sound, we did have a curfew and knew the consequences of being late. The dog apparently didn't realize my haste to get home. In contrast, I read about teenagers today being out at all hours of the night. The fact I read about it in the newspaper means that something bad has happened. If experience teaches us anything, we will admit people who are out and about after 11 p.m. are definitely up to no good, unless they are coming from or going to work.

Many people say they would like to live their lives over, particularly their high school years. Not me! My teen-age years were so full of self-doubt and fear of not being a part of the crowd they should be experienced only once every lifetime. At times a do-over in life might seem like a good idea but only if we are somehow made smarter the second time around and aren't doomed to repeat the same mistakes. However, some of my friends would disagree and they remember those years as the best time of their life. Those were good times but not that good. In fact, the high school years were the worst time of their life for a lot of people. Hopefully, the best days are still ahead of us and have not already passed us by.

God has indeed promised to forgive us of our sins but I don't think he intended to let us forget about them completely. Maybe he leaves us just enough memory to realize how far we have come and just how much farther we have to go. Somehow, the younger generation steadfastly refuses to learn from the mistakes made by their parents and the cycle continues to repeat itself. The fact that parents do not understand the existence of this never ending cycle of misunderstanding only gives credence to what some people call selective memory loss. Does that sound familiar?

The word is out among some of my former high school classmates that I have already written a book and may be in the process of writing another one. Some have considered retaining legal counsel. Fear not, I will not embarrass anyone but myself.

Jackie Hastings

83

Fill'em up George

Shortly after my brother, Johnny, was discharged from the United States Air Force during the 1960's, he began having health related problems which local physicians were unable to diagnose. Our oldest brother, Bill, had already made several visits to Birmingham to see a physician at a highly regarded clinic in the downtown area near UAB. Bill was able to make an appointment for Johnny to see his doctor who quickly diagnosed his problem as adult onset diabetes. After a brief hospitalization, he was able to stop the downward slide of his health issues and stabilize his condition, probably saving his life.

It was about this time that diabetes was found to run in families so several of my brothers, and our father, also became patients of the same doctor at the clinic and generally traveled to Birmingham as a group for our check-ups about two times per year. Normally our father and my brothers, Bill and Johnny, and I would make this trip. On a few occasions our sister, Virginia, and another brother, Bobby, would also schedule an appointment. When this happened, it was necessary to take two cars to accommodate the family. We treated these trips as fun times and an opportunity to be together for a day.

This clinic was staffed then, and is staffed now with some of the finest physicians available anywhere. To this very day, I continue to be a patient at the clinic and my physician is the son of the doctor my family visited thirty years ago. To check for diabetes at that time it was necessary to take a blood sample after fasting for several hours, therefore, we always traveled to Birmingham without eating breakfast. After blood was drawn, we would go around the corner and eat a big breakfast before returning to the clinic for another blood sample and a physical exam. We would then wait to see the doctor and he would go over the results of our exam and various tests. At that time, I was in my late twenties, I always felt intimidated by this doctor because he was so much older, his hair was mostly gray and his demeanor was very direct and to the point. He was sort of blunt, but very polite, and gave me the impression he didn't tolerate a lot of nonsense. One could tell he was a man of faith because of the presence of Bibles on his desk along with an assortment of religious literature. Each session would begin with him saying, "Let me tell you about yourself." He would explain thoroughly the test results and then sort of pass judgment on your health status and always ended the session with, "see you next time." When visiting the doctor without my father and brothers, I would often celebrate my generally good reports by stopping at a Krispy Kreme donut shop which was conveniently located about a block off the interstate near his office.

84

There was an elderly black man working at the clinic whose name was George. He was not a trained nurse or technician of any kind but was always at hand to help out, especially with the male patients of the clinic. After several visits, all of my family became known to George and his duties became quite clear to me on one visit that stands out in my mind to this very day. Daddy questioned me on one occasion if George had asked me to pay my dues. I had no idea what he was talking about until the day my doctor informed me I was to have my colon checked. The term colonoscopy was not yet in my vocabulary as well as it shouldn't have been because of my relatively young age compared to my father and brothers. I was never quite sure why this test was necessary for me but I suspect it had something to do with a chart or a blood sample being applied to the wrong member of my family. The confusion as to which McDonald was which was always evident during our visits. The nurses had to be very careful that the chart in hand actually was the right one for the person they were prepping for a test of any kind. My nightmarish experience on this one particular visit resulted in each of us having to produce our date of birth before any test was performed on future visits.

On this particularly momentous day, I was told by George to put on the dreaded open-backed white gown and strip down to nothing but my socks and follow him. Apparently, socks for an adult are the equivalent of a child's security blanket and can be used to lull the patient into a sense of well-being. That is never good news but I did not want to run afoul of the doctor's orders and I had total confidence in his ability to determine what I needed. However, walking through the halls of a crowded clinic full of patients and nurses wearing nothing but the gown and socks was a humbling experience. The person who decided on this fashion statement found only in a doctor's office was undoubtedly one of the most insensitive people ever to be born. An exhibitionist would be uncomfortable wearing this garment. What could they have been thinking? As I have grown older and more calloused, that sort of experience has become common place and once a person has lost his dignity, it doesn't really matter. However, I did as I was told and meekly followed George into a world that I am thankful no longer exists in the field of medicine, I hope.

During the course of my life there have been so many improvements in medical science they are too numerous to list. No longer do surgeons have to create incisions so gruesome they become as dangerous as the problem they purport to correct. New surgical techniques today have patients on their feet and out the door in a matter of hours. Machines can actually give doctors a look inside the body which practically makes exploratory surgery obsolete. Cancer, while still a dreaded disease, is treatable and curable to the point that only a few short years ago we wouldn't have believed possible. Many years ago I remember leukemia was a death sentence but today it has a ninety percent cure rate. Transplants of the kidney, heart, liver and lung are almost commonplace and have added years to the lives of people who were literally staring death in the face. Severed limbs can frequently be reattached and still retain some degree of usefulness. Medicine has developed joints that can replace worn out knees, hips and shoulders that give the recipient a totally new outlook on life without pain. I can remember as a child the dread in having to go to the dentist and the very real pain that was almost always a part of the visit. Today, a trip to the dentist is totally painless and the advances in that field are enormous.

Since that day at the clinic in Birmingham, I have had several colonoscopies and they are almost non-events. In fact, I sort of enjoy the after effects of the wonderful drug they use to blank out what would otherwise be a very painful experience. The procedure has advanced light years from what it was twenty years ago. As a matter of fact, preparation for the procedure is worse that the procedure itself. It is true the pain is gone but the humiliation remains. It is impossible to maintain one's dignity when faced with an impending colonoscopy. However, what I endured on that day years ago was much more than a loss of my dignity, it was quite painful. In spite of all that, it did have some humorous moments, in hindsight.

The room George led me into was not the type examining room that I was accustomed to seeing. It was not the typical cookie-cutter type room with a table, chair and a few charts on the wall. Instead, there seemed to be a surplus of plumbing fixtures such as sinks, hoses, commodes and a stainless steel table in the middle of the room. There was a long bench outside the door occupied by several men, all wearing the same hideous hospital gown. In addition there was one other factor they all seemed to have in common, they looked extremely sad. They were all much older and their demeanor was much like that of a child waiting to be taken out behind the proverbial woodshed, or maybe even a condemned prisoner waiting to climb the steps to the gallows. Later on, I concluded this poor outlook was the result of some previous experience they must have endured in this very room.

At this point, George turned to me and said "Hmm, I don't believe you've paid your dues, there're in arrears, (this was a partial pun that I didn't understand until later). He added, "You know they call me fill'em up George don't you?" I told him I believed I had heard that title applied to him sometime in the past but didn't understand why. He then explained the necessity of paying dues to join his club. Unlike today, early colonoscopies required the patient to fast the night before and then have their colon cleansed at the doctor's office by actually flushing it out immediately prior to the procedure. A bag, similar to a hot water bottle, was filled with warm water and then forced into the colon through a tube attached to the bag. It was not a lot different than taking a balloon and filling it up with water from a hose. It could be described as sort of water-boarding in reverse. This was apparently one of the duties assigned to George, hence the name, "fill'em up." Those of you familiar with today's procedure will remember that this most unpleasant task is taken care of the night before in the privacy of your own home with the assistance of a very powerful laxative. Ideally, one mixes the laxative with about five gallons of water and, after drinking the mixture, spends the remainder of the night on the commode. However, that important advancement was not yet a widely accepted practice and was probably only in the experimental stage at this very trusting time in my life. So, as I can recall, although through a haze laced with pain and fear of the unknown, the routine was that one mounted the table, assumed a humiliating position, was filled up by George, and then made a mad dash to the closest toilet. It took several cycles of this torture to actually clean the colon enough for the really bad part of the procedure to begin. I was naïve enough to mistakenly believe the water treatment was the really bad part of the procedure.

Now, we can proceed to the matter of the dues and it will make much more sense. George explained that he was the one in charge of deciding when the cleansing part, or water torture, was complete. Unfortunately, those whose dues were in arrears generally took several more cycles than those whose dues were fully paid. This was a practice not unlike executioners of old who demanded payment from their victim so their head could be detached from the body in one swift blow as opposed to something akin to chopping wood for the fireplace. George explained it was hard for him to focus when dealing with someone who didn't pay his fair share. It suddenly became crystal clear to me that I very much wanted to be a fully paid up member of the club.

With that nasty business out of the way, I was taken to another room to await the arrival of the proctologist, which was another new word I learned that day. While waiting, I joined the other extremely sad looking men on the bench. Sometimes you may have noticed that patients waiting in the doctor's office frequently talk with each other and often even laugh. There was no evidence of that type behavior among those of us assigned to the bench and under the care of George.

I am sure the first proctologists were employed in medieval torture chambers but they, like the cockroach, have withstood every effort by mankind to eradicate them to the point of extinction. Unfortunately, they have survived in great numbers. It is extremely difficult to obtain an accurate description of a proctologist because you never actually see their face. One's head would really have to be on a swivel to get a good look at one. Because of this quirk in their professional duties, they are able to remain fairly anonymous and move about freely in our communities.

One by one, the men of the bench were called back into a little room at the end of the hall. As one person was called back to the room, the others slid over to claim their spot because new patients were constantly being added to the end of the bench. Soon, my name was called. Inside the room was a device one might describe as a chair but it did not have a seat like a traditional chair. Two figures stood by the device and one instructed me how to fit myself into it. Remember, the only clothing I had on was the totally worthless open-backed gown and my socks, which were of absolutely no value under the circumstances. More skin would be exposed only in a nudist colony. I am convinced this so-called gown was invented strictly for the purpose of robbing a person of what little dignity they might have left. Also, I firmly believe people clothed in this manner are far less likely to ask frivolous questions, thus the procedure is not prolonged by debate. Something more familiar might be the platform in most drug stores which houses the pharmacist and various underlings. You see, they are purposely on a raised platform, like a king on the throne. This demands respect and puts a damper on any questions. The peons appear one at a time and have to look up to make our pleas for medication. This is all psychological brain-washing. Seriously, how much training do you have to have in order to open a large jar and count out thirty pills?

Since the device had no seat, it was necessary to sort of squat as if you were actually sitting in a real chair. Then, straps were placed across my chest and my arms were strapped to the arms of the chair. For a reason that was soon crystal clear to me, I was told to bring my knees up as close as possible to my chin. When my body reached a level of contortion that apparently suited them, my knees and legs were strapped firmly in place. Then, the entire device was flipped upside down. It was as if I were sitting in an upside down chair with only the straps holding me in. It reminded me briefly of riding the infamous Bullet at the county fair many years ago. However, there was one real difference and that was we actually enjoyed being flipped head over heels while riding the Bullet.

With the gown flopped down over my head, it was difficult to see what was going on up above. One of the attendants kindly explained they were about to visually inspect my colon. My first response was that we really hadn't known each other that long and it

88

would be best to wait a while longer. My plea fell on deaf ears as they seemed to be very intent on getting the process underway. They were undoubtedly concerned about the guys waiting outside on the bench. In order to accomplish this rather intrusive task one of them said they were going to insert a camera attached to a flexible cable and I should remain perfectly still. Seriously, where could I go? If my attorney had been present I am sure an injunction could have been obtained to stop this madness because I had not signed a waiver form. Apparently, they were fresh out of miniature cameras so they used one the approximate size of a shoe box attached to something like a hoe handle. At this point I realized that hanging upside down is good for more than back ailments. Suddenly, my thought process achieved a level of clarity experienced only by a genius. Movies often depict the condemned man shouting, "You've got the wrong man," as he is being led to the gas chamber. Before I could explain that perhaps one of my brothers was the actual intended victim, the procedure was under way and talking was impossible; screaming or incoherent babbling would have been much more appropriate. To describe the process as painful is quite an understatement. As the apparatus snaked its way through my unsuspecting colon it hit a particularly sensitive spot. As my scream echoed through the room and died down, the doctor asked, "How long has that spot been sore?" What a stupid question from a supposedly well educated person. I replied something to the effect that I wouldn't know since this was the first time a camera had ever bumped into it. Under the circumstances, upside down and naked, I thought that was quite a witty response but the man had no sense of humor. I suppose in his line of work he rarely hears a snappy come-back and fails to recognize a good one-liner when he hears it. This begged the question, "Does proctology attract people with no sense of humor or does the nature of the work take it away?" My predicament seemed to go on for hours but I am sure it really lasted only a few minutes. As soon as I was back on my feet, I left the room faster than a scalded dog vacates the back steps.

On the ride home I failed to mention the humiliating experience I had endured. Many years later, my brother Bill and I were reminiscing about our family trips to Birmingham and I told him my deep, dark secret. Much to my surprise, I found out he went through the same ordeal. I was actually overjoyed to hear this because, as they say, misery loves company. My experience also makes me appreciate how far this procedure has come in the last twenty years and it has undoubtedly saved many lives.

I would be remiss if I failed to add that there is no doubt in my mind that George would have lost his job if anyone had any knowledge he was shaking down the clinic's patients for dues. Considering what the man did for a living, he deserved a few extra dollars. Besides, George was such a likable guy no one wanted to rat him out and it does make a good story.

Jackie Hastings

Hiking Tales

The Great Smoky Mountain National Park is the most visited of all the national parks. It is in close proximity of millions of people on the east coast and is not a long distance from the southeastern states bordering the Gulf of Mexico. Like most people, my wife and I began our visits to the mountains by traveling to Gatlinburg, Tennessee, which may be the most well- known destination because of much slick advertising. Unfortunately, what was once a quaint little mountain town has sold its birth-right to developers and has become totally foreign to anything remotely similar to its past. One can stomach only so much glitter and touristy places so we began a transition to campgrounds, rarely ever visiting Gatlinburg. That plastic city is best viewed from the high mountain by-pass as we travel around it. Most campgrounds are surrounded by hiking trails and this was a great way to actually see some of the grandeur never viewed from the asphalt. My guess is that a great majority of the folks who travel to the mountains never actually set foot in the mountains. Most probably never leave the downtown areas and the shopping centers. That is a shame!

Hikers come in many forms, shapes and destinations. The world famous Appalachian Trail passes through the Smoky Mountains and offers the casual hiker an opportunity to hike short sections as opposed to a two thousand mile plus commitment from Springer Mountain in Georgia to Mt. Katahdin in Maine. The most serious of these folks are called thru-hikers and it is their intention to go the entire distance straight through, although few actually make it. This type hiker is easily differentiated from all others because they always smell bad and are grungy in appearance. The smell comes from wearing the same clothes for days at a time and bathing very rarely. Normally, they are not very friendly, especially to those lesser beings they encounter on the trail who hike only short distances at a time and have real jobs to go back to in a real world. Most of us cannot walk away from home, family and a job to spend almost half a year searching for our real self along remote mountain trails. Also, the fact that they are forced to eat a lot of noodles, sleep on the ground and poop in the woods may contribute to their hostility toward other folks with whom they have to share the trail.

Section hikers hike short stretches at a time and come back later for another go at it. Their goal may well be to hike the entire trail but they attempt it for only a few days at a time. Occupying the bottom rung of the hiking hierarchy are the day hikers. These seemingly normal folks hike only during the day time hours and retreat to civilization to spend the night and eat most meals in a restaurant. Day hikers are generally very friendly because they know they will sleep in a real bed at night and not have to fight the rodents and other smelly hikers for space in the shelters regularly spaced the entire length of the trail. Thus, as day hikers, Margo and I began a journey that took us deep into the mountains where we were able to experience vistas most folks only see on a post card or in a travel magazine. It was well worth the effort, at least for me. Margo was a different story and will have to speak for herself.

At this point I must give Margo credit for effort. During the course of our marriage she has made incredible sacrifices for me and, most of the time, I was too stupid to realize that fact. Our hiking exploits were no different. She went along, not because she loved trekking through mountainous terrain with burning lungs and rubbery legs, but because she knew I loved it and was willing to sacrifice her comfort for mine. That fact alone helps to explain why we have been married for almost fifty years.

Our first hike of any consequence took place on a beautiful fall day along a trail originating in Cades Cove. At the far end of what most people call the Loop, we parked at the trailhead and began about a five mile roundtrip hike to a waterfall. The terrain was not steep at all compared to other trails but we were ill-prepared. We failed to carry water or a snack of any kind and most importantly, neither of us had walked five miles in a single day in a long, long time. Well into our hike it became obvious to us there was a big difference between trail miles and mall miles. The final half-mile or so of the trail led us down a descent to the edge of the falls formed by a mountain stream tumbling over a rocky ledge. Our legs had already taken a beating but now the sobering thought of re-tracing our steps stared us squarely in the face.

The hike back began with the uphill climb out of the area of the waterfall. Descending had not been a real problem on the way in but legs already exhausted from the first half of the trip had a very difficult time right off the bat as we climbed up and away from the waterfall. The hike back to our car was hard enough for me but proved to be a nightmare for Margo. She was a real trooper and kept putting one foot before the other. Jokingly, I told her we would have to pay for the helicopter ride if we couldn't make it back to the parking area on foot. The truth of the matter was that there was no flat ground for a chopper to land. By the time we reached our starting point, she was unable to lift her feet into the car. A valuable lesson learned was that if you can't walk five miles, then don't hike two and a half miles because it is always, hopefully, a round trip.

One of the most exciting possibilities when riding around or hiking in the Smoky Mountains is the possibility of seeing a bear in the wild. We had visited the park many times before we actually spotted our first bear. Camping in a bear habitat such as found in campgrounds all over the national park, one has to be aware of their presence and be prudent about certain common sense details. Never hike alone was good advice posted all around the trails. Don't leave food outside. This is very tempting to a bear and they are notorious for raiding campsites and making off with a free meal.

The park rangers give frequent programs for the campers and one of the most popular of the presentations attempts to educate folks on being in close proximity to bears while in the mountains. One thing they stress is for people to be aware of their surroundings and look for the presence of bears. They advise hikers to carry a small whistle in order to make enough noise to frighten a bear. They add that pepper spray could be useful if a bear ventures too close for comfort. Another sage bit of advice is never to try and outrun a bear because it is impossible. They are very fast. After the crowd has been set up for the punch line, the speaker concludes by telling his audience to always be on the lookout for bear droppings. This is a sure sign that bears are probably close by. The ranger already knows that someone in the audience will

Tom and Margo on a back country hike in the Smokey Mountains

always ask how to tell bear droppings from other creatures of the forest. The response it that coyote droppings will always contain bird feathers and squirrel hair while bear

94

droppings smells like pepper spray with a few small whistles mixed in. But the one thing they always stress is that a fed bear is a dead bear. When they lose their fear of humans, sooner or later they will have to be euthanized.

A good beginner's hike is up the mountain trail to Laurel Falls, between the visitor's center outside of Gatlinburg and Townsend. Margo and I were about halfway up the trail when we heard something shuffling around just out of sight along the trail. We decided to be patient and just wait where we were and see if whatever it was came out into plain sight. Sure enough, our patience was rewarded in a few minutes when a rather smallish bear, maybe a hundred pounds, meandered out of the trees, crossed the trail we were on and disappeared down the side of the mountain. Wow! It had happened so quickly we were left standing there with our jaws around our knees. Reality set in a few seconds later when we began to hear shouts and screams as other startled hikers found the bear in their path. A bear viewed from the sanctuary of a car is a lot different situation than face-to-face.

Some people are incredibly stupid around bears and fail to realize they are really wild animals capable of doing a great deal of damage. They are not cuddly teddy bears. This was proven to me a few years ago when we were again in Cades Cove and I happened to see a large, black hump about two hundred yards from the roadway underneath a walnut tree. Anytime a bear is spotted from the road, a bear jam immediately develops. Cars stop in the middle of the road and a crowd gathers quickly. The rangers refer to this scene as a bear jam. By the time others had spotted the bear and the jam developed, I had walked a short distance and saw that it was crunching the walnut shells like they were peanuts. This was a very large bear, probably in the neighborhood of four to five hundred pounds and certainly not approachable. Before I knew what was happening, a fellow blew past me carrying a tripod and an expensive looking camera. It is a good idea not to allow stupid mistakes by other people to define your future so I stopped and slowly began to back away because a confrontation was imminent. The man set up his tripod within a few feet of the bear and began making adjustments to take some close-up pictures. The bear suddenly came to its feet and began a headlong dash toward the startled would-be photographer. If it was a bluff, it was very successful because the man abandoned his equipment and probably set a new speed record dashing back to the safety of his car. The bear returned to his snack of walnuts and I am sure the fellow had a long wait before he could retrieve his camera.

Often we carry a picnic lunch with us and go to one of the isolated areas along the Blue Ridge Parkway and just sit and gaze across the mountains as we enjoy our lunch.

Margo is always very generous and allows me to carry the fried chicken on such excursions. Her theory is that she doesn't have to outrun the bear she just has to outrun me and is counting on the smell of the chicken to lead the bear in my direction.

One glorious Fall day we were seated at a picnic table just off the Blue Ridge Parkway and there was a very old and rustic restroom only a short distance away. The silence was disturbed as a car roared into the nearby parking lot slinging gravel. A woman hustled out of the car and quickly made her way to the old outhouse. One thing we have noticed over the years is that bears can appear suddenly, virtually out of nowhere. One second they are not there and the next second, presto, there is a bear. The lady had only been in the restroom a very short time when we noticed a female bear with two cubs ambling out of the trees toward the room where the woman was obviously seeking relief. The sow bear stopped only a few feet from the door and just stood there with her cubs at her side.

Now, one way to get crossways of a bear real quick is to get between a momma bear and her cubs. To say a bear is over-protective doesn't even come close to describing the situation. It was quickly apparent that the bear was in no hurry to leave and a potentially dangerous scenario was developing only a few feet away from the woman and she didn't know it. There was a small side window in the building almost at roof level and I believed it would be possible to safely make my way to the window and warn the lady and tell her to stay put until the bear vacated the premises. If she had suddenly opened the door it is very likely the bear would have considered her abrupt appearance a threat to her cubs and the lady would probably have had a memory that would last a lifetime and that lifetime could have been very short.

I was able to make my way to the restroom and stood underneath the window and did my dead level best to stave off a looming confrontation with dire consequences. My Good Samaritan moment went something like this:

Me: Lady, can you hear me?

Silence

Me: Lady, can you hear me?

Lady: Go away!

Me: Just listen.

Lady: Who are you?

Me: That's not important, just listen.

Lady: What the (bleep) do you want?

Me: Just listen, I'm trying to tell you something important.

Lady: Get out of here you pervert or I'll start screaming!

Me: Don't open the door, there's a big bear outside.

Lady: You are a sick man, get the (bleep) away from that window!

At this point, discretion became the better part of valor and I walked back to our picnic table and found Margo was missing. She had been around me long enough to know that disaster is my frequent companion and felt the situation was best observed from the security afforded by our locked car. Not taking foolish chances has served her well over the years. Bears can disappear just as suddenly as they can appear and this is exactly what happened. Momma Bear walked briskly back toward the trees and slipped quickly and silently into the surrounding forest.

Perhaps Momma Bear had overheard the venom in the woman's voice and feared for her own safety. Just as the bears disappeared, the restroom door opened about an inch and the woman's eye quickly assessed the situation. Was she looking for me or the bear? Seeing no bear or pervert lurking outside, she swaggered out fully convinced the deviant desires of a redneck sex fiend had been stymied. It would have been a waste of time for me to try to explain what had happened so Margo and I just sat in the car and continued eating our lunch as if we were totally oblivious to the events of the last few minutes. The woman eyeballed me suspiciously as she made her way back to her car just in case she was called upon to pick me out of a police lineup. When she exited the parking lot I observed her vehicle carried a tag from a northern state. This simple act of attention to detail confirmed my worst fears about the intellect of those people. On the other hand, I suspect the feeling was mutual on her part.

One memorable hike Margo and I made was to Andrews Bald. A bald is a clear area high up on a mountain which was not the result of human activity. Many theories abound as to how they occur but the fact is a bald provides a spectacular view of the surrounding mountains because there are no trees to block the scenery. So we drove to the trail head, took up our backpacks with food and plenty of water and roared off down the clearly marked trail. The hike was about three miles and took us more than an hour. Once there, we found a good spot and just marveled at the view. Soon it was time for lunch so we broke out the cans of Vienna sausage, power bars and water and enjoyed a good meal. The day was not hot when we began the hike but had warmed up considerably as the day progressed.

Little did I know but a perfect storm was brewing and it was in Margo's stomach. She has this peculiar trait of becoming nauseous when she sweats. On the way back to the trail head, the combination of greasy sausage sticks, lukewarm water, chocolate and perspiration began to take its toll. We were very close to the end of the hike when she informed me she had to stop for a few minutes. Her face had taken on a pasty, pallid sort of look and her eyes were not focusing properly. I noticed she was sweating profusely and did not seem pleased with my upbeat spirit. It is sometimes difficult for me to figure out exactly what I might be doing that is annoying her and I can only hope to guess correctly. We rested for a few minutes and, at my urging, began the home stretch to the end of the trail. She soon began to lag behind and, like my former football coach, I urged her to move faster.

My exhortations were as unproductive as those of my coach. Practically within sight of the car, she slid slowly to the ground, right where she stood. Unfortunately, the trail we were using is quite popular and other folks were using the trail. Several had to actually step over her prostrate body in order to continue their hike. They seemed quite uncertain as to what they should do as they approached the body lying prone right smack in the middle of the trail.

Apparently trail etiquette covers such an occurrence and each one, without fail, simply slowed and carefully stepped over her body and just kept walking. As for me, I had seen my wife in similar situations and knew she would soon recover sufficiently to get out of the way. While she is in this condition I also knew from experience not to try to move her. Margo does not necessarily believe that misery loves company. In fact, she prefers to be left completely alone. She can get quite caustic when someone makes the mistake of hovering over her so I simply sat on a rock beside the trail and smiled pleasantly at the other hikers as they passed. It has been my experience that when faced with abnormal situations one should try to act as if the event in question is commonplace and is nothing to be concerned about. Sure enough, trooper that she is, she soon struggled to her feet

98

and, after I pointed her in the right direction, wobbled the short distance to the trail's end and slumped across the hood of the car. Wisely, I remained silent knowing her current animosity toward me would soon dissipate. It did seem to be a good idea to let considerable time lapse before I revealed my plans for our next hike.

Another memorable trek in the woods was made in the North Carolina Mountains very close to the campground at the base of the mountain separating that state from Tennessee. The weather had turned very cold and there was considerable snow remaining on the ground from a late Spring, snowfall. Margo does not like cold weather at all thus could not be convinced that she would soon warm up while hiking and all the clothing she had on was excessive. One item in particular was a fuzzy, purple toboggan she insisted on wearing to keep her head and ears warm.

The hike I had in mind was a loop of about five miles which would return us to our starting point. With map in hand, we began in fine spirits, or at least I was in that state of mind and perhaps I should not be putting words in the mouth of my wife. Due to a navigational error on my part, we took a wrong turn and found ourselves much farther up into the mountains than originally anticipated. It was obvious we were off course when the relatively flat route turned into steep uphill climbs. To tell the truth, the obvious change in the landscape did not take a true mountain man to notice the difference. As I had predicted earlier, the excessive attire not only weighed her down but caused her to become uncomfortably warm. We all know that body heat is vented through the top of the head so I recommended she remove the purple head covering. Normally, she doesn't take kindly to my advice but this time it did seem like a good idea. However, when the toboggan was removed much of the purple die, and considerable purple fuzz, remained on her head and framed the perimeter of her face. The hair was plastered to her head from the sweat and practically her whole head and face was dyed purple and accentuated with a lot of the purple fuzz. Since we did not have a mirror with us for her to see how hideous she looked, I stifled an ill-timed laugh and suggested we turn around and go back the way we had come and forget the loop, since we were almost lost.

She wanted to drive on into Cherokee and find a place to eat before returning to our camper. To say that she attracted a good deal of attention when we walked into the restaurant is an understatement of the first order. She seemed somewhat puzzled by the way the waitress kept staring at her and I knew my goose was cooked when she got up and went to the restroom. As I had feared, there was obviously a mirror in the restroom. Upon returning, her appearance had improved greatly but her frame of mind left a lot to be desired. Instead of that distinctly purple hue which had given off a sort of mellow glow, her face was now all red and seemed to be radiating a lot of anger and hostility. All in all, you have to admit it was kind of funny and now, many years later, she actually is able to laugh about the incident.

A very popular hike enjoyed by many is to the Alum Cave Bluff area. The trailhead is located almost to the top of the mountain near the area of New Found Gap. Some of our previous blunders had taught us well so we were properly clothed and supplied for this trip. We had purchased hiking poles, backpacks, and enough assorted paraphernalia to follow Lewis and Clark to the Pacific Ocean if necessary. Our backpacks were stocked with snacks, extra socks, matches, raingear, bandages, splints and snake bite kits.

Of course, we also had plenty of the staple Americans have grown to love and refuse to face life without: toilet paper. The mere mention of toilet paper usually evokes a host of questions from those who haven't spent any time in the woods. Believe it or not, this indelicate topic is generally the focus of many lengthy discussions prior to the beginning of any group hike. Without delving into details, suffice it to say that along with the toilet paper it is highly recommended that hikers carry along a small spade for obvious reasons. If enough time is spent in the woods, believe me there will come a time when it is absolutely necessary to take a short walk away from the trail. When the inevitable does happen, just hope you are not traversing a narrow mountain trail with a sheer drop-off on one side and a steep incline on the other. Women generally have more difficulty with facing this reality and will go to great lengths in an attempt to bring the amenities of home to the wilderness. One such incredible case occurred when I was on an overnight group hike and one lady had her husband carry a portable toilet for her convenience. The poor fellow lugged it all the way to the top of the mountain and back down. Perhaps that is enough information on that topic and we should move on to something else.

Our hike to the Alum Cave area took us alongside a rushing creek, tumbling and leaping over boulders on its merry way down the mountain. Someday, I need to research the question of how a creek manages to find itself on top of a mountain in the first place but that may be the topic of a different story. The trail gradually rose with increasingly slight gains in elevation as we began our approach to the bluff. At one point we struggled on all fours up stone steps someone had graciously carved into huge slabs of rock. Passage through this area would have been very difficult without this thoughtful gesture. We took several breaks along the way, being very careful to keep ourselves hydrated. Finally, we reached the huge bluff standing directly in our path and made our way along its base until we were able to find a way to circumvent the accumulated rocks shed from the bluff face over the centuries. Despite its name, it is not really a cave in the sense we visualize a cave but just a giant overhang under which one could seek shelter if needed.

So, as we sat placidly underneath the overhang, munching on power bars and enjoying the warm glow of victory we felt was so richly deserved by conquering difficult terrain to reach this lovely destination, we began to hear a strange noise, at least strange in these particularly remote surroundings. We heard what sounded like the distinct voices of two people making their way up the same trail we had just traversed. One was apparently a man's voice and the other a woman. It sounded as if they were yelling at each other. The voices continued to make their way in our direction and we sat eagerly anticipating what might be coming up the trail.

The woman came into our line of sight first. She initially appeared as a small blob, sort of like a person on the ground might appear from the top of a tall building. When she finally got close enough to pick out details, we were both amazed at what we were seeing. In contrast to our hiking garb, this woman looked like she had just left a church service or a funeral. She was dressed to the hilt, as some would say. She was wearing a miniskirt and high heels with a purse over her arm. Her male companion soon emerged from the trees and was maybe several hundred yards behind Eileen. We knew that was her name because the man was repeatedly shouting for Eileen to stop. Instead of stopping, Eileen took the fork in the trail which would eventually lead her up to where we were sitting. On the other hand, the man stayed on the lower trail and was adamant that she stop walking.

There was obviously a dispute in progress and it had become very public, although there was not much of a public to witness the event. By the time she arrived at our perch, she was probably a hundred feet above him and seemed to have no intention of obeying his instructions to stop. As they moved past us, we could hear him continue to shout, "Eileen, get the (bleep) down here." Eileen never acknowledged our presence and we knew better than to get involved in a domestic dispute. This one-sided conversation continued until they were well beyond our range of hearing. The disturbing thing was that they were headed higher and deeper into the mountainous terrain and did not appear to have any water or snacks.

Our pride at having successfully traversed such difficult terrain was dampened immensely by the fact that Eileen had made the same trip in patent leather pumps, a nice attractive miniskirt, an expensive looking top of some kind while lugging around a purse. Her friend obviously considered her worth pursuing into the wilderness. Our successful trek into the wilds of the mountains had been up-staged by Eileen and her partner. During the remainder of our stay in the mountains I diligently watched the nightly news for some word of a missing woman by that name. However, no word came and her fate remains a mystery to us. When we related this tale to our friend Billy Heard, he began calling my wife, Eileen, and did so until the day he passed away many years later.

The many times Margo and I were able to hike in the mountains remain a very pleasant memory to me but, in hindsight, maybe not so pleasant to her. But, if we can't accept the fact that things change, whether we want them to or not, our life will take a turn for the worse. We must be careful not to let the past consume the future. But when the muscles stopped aching and the sweat and purple dye disappeared down the shower drain, our forays into the mountains left us with a lifetime of memories and laughs. Even more importantly, it left us with a greater awe of what God has created and left in our care.

The author taking in the view from a favorite vantage point on the Blue Ridge Parkway.

Jackie Hastings

A Day at Arlington

      I had been to Arlington National Cemetery on several occasions as a tourist. All the familiar sites had been visited many times: President Kennedy's grave, the changing of the guard at the Tomb of the Unknowns, the Marine Corp Memorial and the Custis-Lee Mansion. On this day, I was much more than a tourist, I was on a mission. With my wife, Margo, and our daughter, Amy, we were searching for my Uncle Claud Lindsey's grave site among the thousands of veterans buried at this very special place. We had a few hours late in the afternoon before we were to attend an Honor Flight program at the World War II Memorial in downtown Washington, D. C. Our daughter was the co-director of the Honor Flight Program in the Birmingham area and her mother and I had promised her we would attend one of the events before the waiting list was exhausted and the program brought to a conclusion. Over a period of several years this group was able to transport almost 1000 World War II veterans from the Birmingham area to visit their memorial in Washington. On this particular trip our daughter rode with us from home and planned to return to Birmingham with the veterans on the chartered flight.

Tom and Margo searching for Uncle Claud's grave at Arlington National Cemetery.

My Uncle Claud was my mother's brother, the eighth out of nine children, and the youngest of four sons of Leonard and Lucy Lindsey, my grandparents. The phrase, "a rolling stone gathers no moss" was coined to describe the life my uncle evidently chose to lead. He left his parent's home in East Florence with apparently no intention of ever returning, except for very brief visits spread out over very long intervals. Most of my other uncles took the same road to the military but always returned to their home whenever possible for joyful reunions on special occasions. The Lindsey side of my family was not one to freely share information and perhaps there was a reason for him to leave home and return so infrequently but it was not a topic of conversation in my presence.

My older brothers, Bill and Joe, were separated in age from Claud by only a few years and they sort of grew up together. Our grandfather, Leonard Lindsey, ran a store in East Florence for many years. All of his sons, my brothers, and some of our cousins, spent a great deal of time at the store working and just hanging out hoping to get a chance to drive Poppa's old delivery truck, a 1919 Ford. During those years, late 30's and early 40's, few people had transportation of their own and most of them would certainly not have used their precious gas and tires to drive to the store. Instead, they phoned in their grocery order to be delivered, sort of like Lum and Abner on their popular radio show many years ago. It would seem Poppa Lindsey kept a good segment of the young men in East Florence out of trouble by using them as delivery boys. The opportunity to drive the old delivery truck was a great treat to teenage boys and was their opportunity to learn to drive. There is no doubt that once the old truck left the store it traveled to places Poppa never imagined and, consequently, never shared with him for obvious reasons.

Both my brothers have passed along to me many memories they have of growing up with their uncles, Poppa Lindsey's sons, and working for our grandfather. My cousin Charles McDonald, the same age as my brother Joe, told me of one humorous event he had while working at Poppa's store. For some strange reason that can't be explained, every boy in our community had the habit of sticking his thumb in a soft drink bottle and making a popping noise after the top was removed. Then, if we had an extra nickel, we poured in a bag of salted peanuts. This was not a widespread practice because most of the people I have talked with have never heard of anyone doing that in other places. Anyway, Poppa's store was directly across the road from a large knitting mill and many of the workers came to his store during lunch or after work. On this particular day, a woman came in and wanted a Nu-Grape drink. Trying to be helpful, my cousin quickly fished one out of the gigantic cooler, popped the top with the bottle opener on the cooler, stuck his thumb in the top of the bottle to make the desired sound and handed it to the lady. She refused to take it because he had stuck his thumb in in. Charles got her another Nu-Grape and drank the one she considered to be contaminated by his thumb. Come payday, Poppa deducted a nickel from my cousin's earnings to pay for the drink. That was vintage Poppa Lindsey.

My Uncle Claud was a career military man, entering the United States Army Air Corp in 1943. This aerial branch of the U. S. Army later became the modern day United States Air Force after World War II. He was shipped out to England where he served as a tail gunner aboard a B-26 bomber. During one of many bombing runs over Germany, he was wounded and awarded the Purple Heart. While Claud was recuperating from his wounds in England, my brother Joe joined the Navy and lost contact with Claud for many years. The next time they saw each other was in 1964 when our mother passed away. After Korea, Claud managed to see further action in a hot spot in Asia during the Vietnam War very few people knew existed; more about this later. As Claud moved from one duty station to another across this country and the world, he left ex-wives and children scattered in his wake. Some of his children surfaced from time to time looking for a connection to family their wandering father never provided. They were searching for names of paternal grandparents, aunts, uncles and cousins they knew probably existed but had no idea who they were or where to look. Some piece of information usually led them to north Alabama and eventually to the door of my oldest brother, Bill, who was the family historian. Over the years, Bill spent a tremendous amount of time corresponding and visiting with our various relatives, some of them children of our uncle Claud. His book, _Judi Letters_, is a recounting of the letters written to Claud's daughter, Judi, in an attempt to fill in the gaps about family she never knew. Our cousin, Judi, eventually visited Florence and became acquainted with a host of her relatives. Unfortunately, the connection was made so late most all of her aunts and uncles had already passed away.

The trip to Arlington to search for Claud's grave was an effort on my part to fulfill a last request of my oldest brother. As a retired colonel in the Army Reserve, and having served as an Army Chaplin, he had traveled to Washington in 1994 to conduct our uncle's funeral. Bill had been asked to do this final favor by Claud, or maybe one of his children, when the time came. There was only five years difference in their ages so Bill and Claud, despite being uncle and nephew, spent considerable time roaming the neighborhood and playing together. Both spent many years in the military but my brother maintained his roots and family connections while Claud did not. This boyhood connection and the fact that Claud was our mother's brother were reason enough for Bill to make the long trip to Washington for a very short funeral service. There are so many funerals at Arlington in one day, about 100 per week, each individual funeral is scheduled within a very specific block of time and one party has to clear out so the next funeral can begin. Because of this limited time frame, my brother was not able to stay and see the closing of the grave or the headstone erected. He wanted very much to see a picture of Claud's grave marker in the total context of all the other graves around it in our national cemetery. Failing health prevented him from returning over the next several years.

Thus, that explains why we were traipsing around the cemetery, camera in hand, looking for a needle in a haystack. That pretty much describes the way it was. We had some rudimentary information on Claud and went to the visitor's check-in desk to get the exact location of the grave. That turned out to be wishful thinking. They could not give us the exact location of his grave, only a general area in which to search. At that time the information was not computerized but kept on 3 X 5 index cards which had to be thumbed through manually. The complete absence of a computerized record keeping system was very surprising to me. Apparently, there was more than one veteran with the name Claud Lindsey buried at Arlington and the clerk on duty had considerable difficulty giving us any usable information. He could only give us several possibilities and based on the day of birth and death, one stood out from the others. We were able to obtain the general area where the grave was located and set out on foot to begin our search. That problem has apparently been remedied because today, only a few short years later, one can access a gravesite with the proper computer equipment and obtain photos of the marker while seated at your desk at home.

The only vehicles allowed within the confines of the cemetery were those belonging to family members attending a funeral and the tour vehicles going to the Tomb of the Unknown Soldier and the Kennedy gravesite. Everyone else had to hoof it. After a somewhat lengthy search, we finally located the site and took plenty of pictures as evidence of our success.

During the time we were standing around my uncle's grave, another burial was taking place on a knoll across the way. It was a very moving experience to stand in the midst of our nation's premier military cemetery and hear the twenty-one gun salute and taps being played for another veteran whose time on this earth had expired. The slight breeze on the crisp October day carried the sounds all across the hallowed ground at our feet and made me even more aware that I was in the midst of many of our nation's greatest heroes. As far as I could see in any direction, I was looking at a sea of white headstones, all perfectly in line with each other in all directions. The story behind almost every marker was a story that was part of the building blocks of our nation. The men and women buried at Arlington represent the best this country had to offer, not only to the citizens of their own country but to the whole world. The feet of these veterans trod the ground of virtually every battle field this planet has known since the birth of the United States. It occurred to me we were standing not just in a cemetery, but we were in the midst of the greatest accumulated sacrifice that mere mortals have ever made, probably in the history of the world. If we took away the sacrifice made by the people buried on these few hundred acres, our nation would be far less successful as the world's greatest experiment in self-rule by free people. The entire world has been the beneficiary of what these individuals were willing to do for their country. I wonder sometimes if the world remembers or appreciates the blood this nation has spilled on their behalf. No other nation in the world has been willing to shed its blood and treasury in order for other people to enjoy the benefits of a free society. It would be even worse if the people of our own nation ever allowed the memory of this same sacrifice to disappear from the national conscience. The sacrifice of these people in the performance of their duty is the paper on which the history of the United States of America is written. It takes a lot of heroes to fill up a national cemetery but this nation has produced enough to do just that. Because of space limitations, it now takes virtually an act of Congress to secure a burial spot on this hallowed ground.

After a long but successful search, Claud's grave was finally located among the many thousands at Arlington.

My mother never seemed to know where her brother was at any given time. His visits were as unpredictable as they were infrequent. Claud might come through town and visit one brother or sister and the rest would never know he was anywhere around. One Saturday morning in the 1970's, I was delivering a used sofa to the Salvation Army building in East Florence. Much to my surprise, the man who helped unload it was my uncle Claud. He didn't recognize me but I immediately recognized him. We talked for a little while but eventually he had to get on with his job. He stayed only a few more days before leaving town ahead of any contact with other family members. Claud had apparently been in town several weeks and none of his kin knew he was anywhere around. His will-of-the-wisp life style went to extremes when my mother died in 1964. My brother, Joe, picked him up in Oklahoma City on his way home for the funeral. The day of the funeral arrived and Claud was nowhere around, he had already left town. He was not willing to stay a few more hours in order to attend the funeral of his sister. At the time, this bothered me much more than it should have. Still in high school, I had little knowledge of the ups and downs of life and could not fathom the same happening on the McDonald side of my family. I resolved that someday I would bring this up with my uncle if I ever had an opportunity.

That day did not arrive until almost twenty-five years had passed. By that time, my anger was long gone. From 1983 until 1991, I traveled to Washington very frequently on business with the National Education Association, which is headquartered in our nation's capital. My brother Bill had discovered Claud was living in the Soldier's Home, also in our capital, and asked me to visit him if I ever had time. This home provides a permanent residence for certain retired military veterans. The main building was built in 1851 and served as a summer residence for President Lincoln when he wanted to escape the heat and humidity and favor-seeking crowds of downtown Washington. The entire facility covers several hundred acres and is actually a city within a city, providing almost every need, from recreation to medical services, to its residents.

My meeting adjourned early on one Saturday afternoon and this gave me an opportunity to visit my uncle. After a rather lengthy taxi ride through a really bad part of town, I arrived at the gate of the Soldier's Home. The guards directed me to the cafeteria building where they said Claud was employed for a few hours each day. He had no idea I was coming and was summoned by speaker to the lobby of the building where I was waiting. A few minutes later, a man came walking down the hall and I immediately recognized as my uncle Claud. He appeared to be very surprised to see me after I introduced myself but, seemed to be genuinely glad I had come to visit. We sat in the lobby for a few hours and talked about family and how our hometown had changed over the years. He seemed to know much more about my childhood than I would have thought and we laughed at some of the things he remembered about me and my brothers and sister. We were raised only a few dozen feet from each other and we knew the same people and the same places but we were generations apart in more than just years. His health was not good and it showed in his face. The topic of his absence at my mother's funeral did not seem important to me while talking to a man who appeared to be beaten down by a lot of things much more important. Claud had suffered much tragedy since that day in 1964. His oldest son, Richard, was a school administrator in Muncie, Indiana, and witnessed his fifteen year old son attacked and killed by another student in the hall at the high school where he served as principal. One of his daughters had been murdered in Montgomery by a random drive-by shooting while she was on her way to work. As the sun set on that visit, he informed me that if I was going to go back to my hotel, I had better hurry and call a cab. Taxi drivers refused to come into that neighborhood after dark. Plainly, Washington, D. C. and Cloverdale, Alabama, are separated by more than miles. Experience has taught me a lot of bad things take place after dark, so that seemed like good advice to follow. The visit was a good one and I was very glad I came. The hurt feelings of long ago had mysteriously vanished.

We visited many more times over the next few years and he talked a lot about his life in the military. He revealed to me that he took part in the Air America operation, which smuggled spies, sabotage teams, war casualties, visiting VIPs, and many other things, all over Southeast Asia during the Vietnam War. This was a totally clandestine operation funded by the CIA and supposedly unknown to Congress. His role was to serve as a navigator aboard one of the converted aircraft which landed, sometimes under fire, in jungle air strips to hurriedly unload their cargo and be on their way as quickly as possible. The men who volunteered for these missions were sort of modern day swashbuckling adventurers who were generally retired military or CIA operatives. Many books and motion pictures are available chronicling this extremely covert organization.

My last visit with my uncle had a rather prophetic ending. As he walked with me outside to meet my taxi, I told him I would visit again on my next trip in a couple of months. He looked at me and said, "Tommy, I won't be alive when you come back." Claud was a tough guy and his record of service to our country proves it, but on this occasion, he was as close to being emotional as he could be without actually shedding tears. I hugged him before leaving, and the last time I saw him he was standing in the driveway watching the taxi pull away. My uncle Claud died a short time later.

The author placed his brother's picture and the American flag which draped his coffin in front of the Alabama marker at the World War II Memorial in Washington, D.C. Bill desperately wanted to visit the site on an Honor Flight but was too ill.

Roots seem to be important to a lot of us while others have sort of a tumbleweed mentality. I am not talking about work and military obligations. Those commitments are a necessary part of living. I am talking about our connections with family. There is no doubt the fact that many folks had no qualms about pulling up stakes and setting out for parts unknown led to the westward expansion and eventual coast to coast settlement of this great nation. Roots are important to me and always have been. I want a place called home and for my family to be a part of a community where people know us and we know them. I have never been willing to forsake old friends just to go out and find new ones. The theme song to the popular television show, *Cheers*, had a line which described a place, "where everybody knows your name." As dull as it may sound, that is sort of the way I operate. But people are different and it is amazing how people in the same family, raised by the same parents, with the same neighbors and with the same friends are in this regard.

My wife's father led much the same kind of life as my uncle Claud. Her parents divorced early in her life and she never really knew her father. He bounced from place to place and job to job and she rarely knew where he was for years at a time. Out of the blue one day, she received a call from a hospital in Chicago. He had died alone, much as he had lived, far from friends and family.

Maybe the wanderers of the world, like my uncle and Margo's father, outwardly sever their physical roots but their heart still remembers a place, or person, that continues to connect them to what they consider to be home. Maybe home is not a physical place at all but a state of well-being and acceptance. No matter what an individual considers home to be, the Bible tells us this world is not our final resting place and our life is nothing more, in regard to time, than a whiff of smoke and then it is gone. The soul of every man, woman and child has a final home and it is not of this world. Regardless of how far our steps may carry us from our physical home; there is always one last step to take to reach our final destination.

Joys of Camping

It was obvious trouble was brewing when I noticed steam coming from under the hood. My wife and I were headed for the Smoky Mountains: Cades Cove to be more exact. We were to meet some friends there and hopefully enjoy a few days wallowing in the beauty of the great outdoors. The excitement over this trip had been building for so long it had obviously affected our thought process so we were determined to press on despite minor mechanical problems like an over-heated radiator. To make matters even worse, it was the third Saturday in October and every football fan worth their salt knows that is always the day Alabama and Tennessee meet in football. We were stuck halfway up a mountain in Chattanooga waiting for a wreck to be cleared off the interstate somewhere ahead of us. This had created the radiator problem because we weren't moving forward at all and idling creates no air flow to cool the radiator. The fact we were towing a six thousand pound camper with a one-half ton pickup only complicated our problem.

My knowledge of towing a camper was very incomplete and it did not take me long to figure out it was far different than towing the horse trailer of my younger years. Towing was a word I only started using since I bought the camper. Before, I simply said I was pulling a trailer. It wasn't long before I stopped saying camper and started using the term, recreational vehicle, or RV for short. It is much easier to say and a lot easier to spell. The truck I was driving while stranded on the side of the mountain was totally unfit to tow a heavy load but I had no clue. I believe it was rated to tow nothing heavier than a two-wheel trailer hauling a lawn mower. Later I was to learn about heavy duty shocks in the rear, extra capacity radiators and a cooling unit for the transmission. Some trucks have a certain gear ratio built in at the factory that makes towing much easier on the vehicle. The camper attached to our bumper was built in 1968, and was probably as unfit to tow as was the truck. At times, ignorance can be bliss.

Things can certainly go wrong while pulling a horse trailer but they can go very wrong towing an RV. A horse trailer could have a flat tire or break an axle or the horse could get turned around and jump out the back. Unless you were hauling a pair of Belgians, a flat tire on a double-axle trailer might not put you out of service. A flat tire on an RV would probably blow out the other tire on that side, because of the added weight, and cause it to lean toward "Aunt Fronie's house" as my daddy was fond of saying. An RV can actually catch fire and burn while it is being towed. We witnessed just such a startling event one day while my wife and I were traveling east on I-40. The camper was being towed by a SUV headed down Roan Mountain. The day had almost turned to night and to us, it looked sort of like a comet as it streaked down the mountain and blazed past going in the opposite direction. Maybe they were trying to outrun the fireball but for certain, their trip was ruined. Be that as it may, we did finally make it to Cades Cove that day which was proof that the Lord still watches over idiots. The mere fact that I am still here to write these words is all the proof needed.

Towing a heavy RV can be hazardous in many ways but it is also sort of like planning ahead in a game of chess. It can be extremely stressful because one has to think so far ahead to avoid getting into a bad predicament. Stopping for fuel while driving a car is a no-brainer requiring little advance planning. However, it is very difficult while towing a camper because of the wide turn space it requires to move the RV into and out of close proximity to the pump for the hose to reach the tow vehicle. Very few gas stations are built to accommodate vehicles under tow. In addition, fast food establishments are not equipped for a tow vehicle and an RV because together, some will measure close to fifty feet in length. Certainly, taking advantage of a drive-through for a quick meal is out of the question. Forget about parking the rig to go inside. Sudden lane changes are also a no-no and at times, one has to travel several miles to find an appropriate place to turn around. This always happened when Margo, with the map in her lap, would turn to me and say, "I think you should have turned back there." However, there is one good thing about towing an RV: there is always a bathroom right behind you.

In the meantime on this particular day, Peyton Manning was killing us over in Knoxville. While the massacre was taking place we were surrounded by scores of Tennessee fans and we were driving a truck which had a Roll Tide tag on the front bumper, a crimson Alabama flag attached to the window and appeared to have a fire under the hood. By the time we got started up again our ears were burning from all the abuse being heaped upon us by folks in cars with orange flags attached. It was unclear whether they were more amused by the game or the fact we were driving around in a truck which might be on fire. The situation in Knoxville kept getting worse and the abuse around us increased in direct proportion to the score. Coach Bryant always said Tennessee fans had no class and all Tide fans knew for a fact he was never wrong.

Over the years I have learned from experience a couple of other flaws Coach Bryant should have added to his list: narrow mindedness and a poor sense of humor are two which immediately come to mind. During one visit to the mountains, my wife and I were out driving around, as we like to do, and we stumbled across a large Wal-Mart in Newport, Tennessee. Now it is a well-known fact that campers love Wal-Mart. We have visited Wal-Mart stores from Pascagoula, Mississippi, to Front Royal, Virginia, and many points in between. There is an unwritten axiom among campers to avoid any city which does not have one of Sam Walton's creations. Since they are open twenty-four hours a day it's always an option to park in their enormous parking lot and spend the night while traveling. This not only removes the headache of maneuvering a camping rig while searching for a real campground, but also avoids the camping fee for one night. Also, one can go inside and actually shop around at two in the morning if sleep is hard to come by. Inside this store in Newport, there was a sea of orange t-shirts proudly displayed at every turn. Such a disgusting sight inspired me to ask the associate for a crimson red Alabama shirt. She acted as if she had just gotten word of a dead skunk in aisle fifteen. Rather haughtily she was quick to inform me that they did not carry any shirts other than those with the University of Tennessee logo. As we were being escorted out of the store by security, I let it be known that the Wal-Mart store in my hometown in North Alabama stocked Tennessee, Vanderbilt and even Auburn shirts, in addition to Alabama shirts. Their refusal to stock Alabama gear was the epitome of narrow mindedness and I intended to let Sam Walton know about the kind of narrow-minded people he had running this particular store.

Another serious flaw was revealed to me when my wife and I traveled to Columbia, Tennessee, to visit their annual Mule Day celebration. By the way, this is something well worth seeing, even if you don't like mules or being around Tennessee fans. It is quite an experience to observe both, mules and Tennessee fans, in close proximity to each other. The similarities are much more obvious. But anyway, people come from such far away nations as New York City to take in this event and it is indeed a marvel to behold. As we walked around and viewed some of the inside vendor's wares, I saw a poor fellow dressed entirely in orange. He had an orange hat on his head, an orange shirt, pants, socks and even orange shoes. I casually inquired if he had dressed early that morning while it was still dark? He said he had not and wondered why I had asked what seemed to be a silly question. I responded something to the effect that a sane person would never knowingly dress as he was if he could see himself in a mirror. His harsh response was proof that people of his ilk were totally devoid of a sense of humor. Of course, Coach Bryant had been gone a long time and it was now payback time for the weak sisters of the poor. Coach Bryant also believed it was as important to show class as a winner as it was as a loser. It is difficult to exhibit class when winning if such an event is rarely experienced. Apparently, the good people of our neighboring state did not appreciate Coach Bryant's wisdom.

One of my favorite jokes for years was to announce to the few people who listened to my foolishness that the legislatures of both Alabama and Tennessee were considering a bill to merge and form one state. The obvious reason was that the people in Alabama had always wanted to have an Opryland amusement park and the people of Tennessee always wanted to have a good football team. The joke generally earned a few good chuckles around Alabama fans and was very relevant for many years but time changes things. At the time of our ordeal of being stranded halfway up the mountain, both Opryland and a good Alabama football team had disappeared in the rear-view mirror, so to speak. The Alabama football team was regularly turning victory into defeat and causing their loyal fans to wonder why their world had turned upside down.

Meanwhile, the amusement park at Opryland had vanished from the face of the earth. One can almost understand the fortunes of a football team waning and rising with time, those things are inevitable in life. But, good grief, who in their right mind would tear down the best family amusement park in the northern hemisphere to replace it with a shopping mall? No more joining up with our best friends and packing our kids in the back of a pickup with some lawn chairs and a bottle of water and traveling to Nashville to spend a few tourist dollars. Actually, we spent very few dollars because we always took along enough friend chicken and potato salad to feed all of us for days. Lunch was always eaten in the parking lot beside the river. Teachers with a family of four could not afford to eat lunch in an amusement park anywhere, not even Nashville. In the spirit of fairness, the high price of food is something all such destinations have in common. If you don't believe it, try a burger and fries at Dollywood.

By the way, my wife and one of her friends packed all four kids in the back of a pickup one summer, with the luxury of a bed cover of course, and went to Dallas, Texas, to visit her parents. They had sleeping gear, water and snacks and had a great time. As adults, the kids still talk about the trip when they get together. I am quite sure such fun things are now against the law.

However, all these frightening things which can occur while en route pale in comparison when it comes to actually backing the entire rig into a space designed for campers of the 1930's and 1940's. Cades Cove is an older campground, established around the time the park was opened during the 1930's. Campers at that time were tiny in comparison and many campers slept in their cars or in tents. Be that as it may, we once witnessed a guy towing a rather large sailboat pull into a campground and use the boat for a camper. Another time we camped next to a man and woman camping out of a stretched limousine. Today's pickups and RV's can be extremely large and difficult to maneuver in tight areas. All the newer drive-through type sites are reserved for the huge motor homes and the older sites are frequently all that is left for the peons towing campers. These require the unit to be backed into the space and this can be very problematic.

Backing for the average person is not a natural function, particularly when one is driving a fifty foot unit hinged in the middle. Many of today's campers will not go to a campground unless they can pull directly into a camp site. They will travel hundreds of miles to avoid having to back a large RV. Their policy seems to be to only move forward. There is probably a good life lesson somewhere in this philosophy: while traveling the highways and byways of life while towing all of life's heavy burdens behind us, we should strive to move forward, not backward. Unfortunately, such a deep and meaningful thought has no place in this story. Some campgrounds are designed to make this easy, Cades Cove is not. For some strange reason, esthetics I suppose, they have placed refrigerator-sized boulders around the campground. I would love to have some of these rocks in my yard but they are pretty much in the way while trying to back into a narrow space. While using mirrors, which actually have printed on their surface a warning that distances can be deceiving, one must slip the camping unit past a boulder on one side while simultaneously avoiding bashing a front fender into another elephant-sized boulder as the truck makes a ninety degree turn in reverse. This requires a deft touch not normally found in the general public.

Watching this play out is actually very amusing to the campers already in place with nothing else to keep them occupied. They have already, miraculously in some cases, managed to get their own RV into the site and set up and are extremely busy doing nothing. They have taken their punishment and can't wait to see someone else get theirs. It can be compared to a bunch of unruly boys in school lining up for a paddling. Always go first and then some of the pain goes away when you have the pleasure of watching your cohorts as they make their way to the front of the line.

If a camper already in residence happens to notice a new arrival slowly making his way to a nearby campsite, it is generally with great anticipation of a pending dramatic comedy. If the driver happens to be a seasoned camper and has the RV in place in a flash, there is a lot of disappointment. The show is over before it begins. However, if the driver leaves the RV in the road, walks back while scratching his head and his wife is out and pointing at various obstacles, there is a good possibility a brouhaha is about to ensue before your very eyes. All heads within the immediate area will turn to watch what is about to happen. There are many people on the staff in a national park. There are wildlife managers, biologists, botanists, environmental specialists, park rangers and others.

118

However, I believe there should always be one more person assigned to the campground. No, I do not mean a divorce lawyer but, instead, a marriage counselor. A marriage that can survive years of camping and the hazards associated with backing an RV into a campsite in a national park can survive almost anything.

The failure to communicate has been identified as the culprit in many of the misunderstandings we have on a daily basis. This breakdown can occur in any environment where people are together and a successful outcome depends on each knowing and understanding what the other is trying to say. At a campsite, the scenario is very predictable. Generally, the male is the driver and the female is the passenger whose role is always to get out of the tow vehicle and help guide the RV into the campsite without damaging the camper, the truck, or any portion of the facilities. Drivers who drive eighteen wheelers and back the trailers into tight areas usually do so with a little help from someone behind the trailer who is giving hand signals. The same is true with campers. However, in order for hand signals to work, the one doing the signaling must be visible to the driver. This rather simple task is normally accomplished by standing in a position which can be observed by the driver as he looks through the mirrors attached to the sides of the vehicle. For some reason, many women fail to comprehend this very basic rule and tend to wander around somewhere behind the RV totally out of the line of sight of the driver. So many women behave in this manner it almost makes me believe it is genetic. They may be using the best hand signals known to mankind but if they are not visible, it is a hopeless situation. This tends to anger the driver and his shouts can be heard coming from the cab, much to the delight of all the onlookers. My wife tells me that the woman is simply trying to watch both sides and must wander back and forth constantly yelling "wait, wait," to a driver who cannot hear what is being said behind him and out of sight. On a personal experience, I have actually backed our RV into an obstacle at the rear of the camper only to hear my wife say, "That's far enough." To help alleviate this vexing problem, my wife and I once purchased a pair of walkie-talkies so we could communicate better and the line of sight problem would cease to be an issue. We actually realized the severity of the problem and took preventative action. However, it didn't work as planned. I found it extremely difficult to turn the steering wheel while pressing the send button on the unit while simultaneously watching for boulders and trees in the front of the truck. I believe we used our walkie-talkie only one time before I threw mine out the window.

The scenario described above is generally resolved in one of two ways. The first being the man instructs the female to get back in the truck and they drive away, both in a state of rage and, quite possibly, seeking a divorce lawyer. Hopefully, they are seeking a pull-through site or possibly returning to their home with the camping trip being summarily cancelled. A better solution to the problem is for one of the onlookers, preferably a man who knows what kind of information the driver needs, to step forward and relieve the wife of the tremendous responsibility of preventing damage to their camper. It is extremely important not to suggest trading places with the driver. This is very damaging to the male ego, particularly in front of his wife, and would place the driver in a situation which would do tremendous damage to his self-esteem. With competent assistance, the RV is generally in place within a matter of minutes, if not seconds. The wife disappears mysteriously and is apparently being consoled by other compassionate wives in the vicinity. She suddenly reappears when the deed is done. Couples who have been married many years immediately go about their business as if this ugly incident never occurred. Among other couples, there is discernable tension at the campsite.

Since most campgrounds are in dire need of revenue they arrange the sites to accommodate as many RV's as possible. The result is that the campers, who, for the most part, are total strangers, are generally forced to live in very close proximity for a period of time over a few days to a few weeks. Most every place we have ever camped had a site for what is known as the campground host. This job is generally taken by a retired couple with many years of camping experience and the wisdom of Solomon. Their main responsibility is to see that everything runs smoothly and to try and settle minor differences between campers. In return, they are generally given the best campsite free of charge along with other perks such as a water, sewer and electrical hookups along with cable television, if available.

While in college I was forced to read a book entitled, **Territorial Imperative**. The gist of the required reading was that all creatures have a space which must be respected by other creatures. Most mammals will protect this territory, some much more fiercely than others. For example, a grizzly requires a lot of space. If you get into his space, the result is frequently a disaster for the intruder. None of us want someone else to get in our face, so to speak.   When another person gets too close to us while talking, we generally become very uncomfortable because they are violating the unwritten law of intruding on our territory. One axiom of living a good and long life is that we should always be wary of intruding on the space of others. This is also true at a campground.

The most frequent violators of another camper's space are children and pets, especially dogs. Camping is a great family activity and the opportunity to take the kids to the outdoors for a vacation is a great learning experience for the entire family. However, when a passel of kids with bikes are nestled right next to a retired couple who want only peace and quiet, sparks can fly. There is a very nice campground in Andrews, North Carolina, which specifically prohibits children. We know this to be true because there is a huge sign at the entrance boldly displaying the words, "No children allowed." The sign is placed there for the benefit of grandparents who refuse to believe the child of their child would be considered obnoxious by other people. However, the child's parents know full well how obnoxious their own kids can be and that is the reason they have sent them off with their grandparents for some time in the great outdoors. Children have many flaws and one is a tendency to chase each other constantly and then take short cuts to get to where they want to go. In doing so, they often zip across another campsite, thus violating the space of their neighbor. It is not unusual to see older folks rope off their entire campsite in order to keep the children away.

Pets are even more annoying than children. Nothing spoils a good night of relaxing sleep quite like a dog in the camper next door howling like a banshee. And that is not all. It goes far beyond annoying to step outside your RV early on a crisp, fall morning in the mountains and step squarely into a huge pile of dog poop deposited during the night. The campground host is frequently called upon to settle these type problems and thus earn all the free perks.

Children and dogs are not the only reasons friction can ruin a good camping trip. People who are simply rude and inconsiderate can be even worse. There is a free campground on the Natchez Trace near Hohenwald, Tennessee, that came very close to being the site of an international incident involving locals and foreigners. It is the site where the famous explorer, Meriwether Lewis, died and is buried and thus the surrounding park bears his name. It is a free campground because the federal government has to have a certain number of free camping sites and Meriwether Lewis Campground serves this purpose. No water, sewer or electrical hookups are available and it is quite primitive. However, it is very beautiful, especially in the spring and fall with its rolling hills, wildflowers and abundant streams and wildlife. The sites are also very far apart and it is a very nice place to spend a few days, especially on the weekends, for local campers in the area.

A problem arises every year involving Canadian campers who suddenly swarm in and take up all the available spaces, leaving no room for the locals. My wife and I met a very gracious couple from Montreal who explained the situation to us. It seems that for Canadian citizens to qualify for the national health insurance program it is necessary to spend a minimum of six months in country. However, many prefer to spend the cold

121

winter months on the Texas Gulf Coast. This is quite understandable behavior for people who live in a nation whose only contribution to their southern neighbors has been a history of producing cold fronts which make us miserable and an obsession with the strange game of ice hockey. Any southerner who understands the game of ice hockey has not lived in the Deep South very long. The Natchez Trace takes these migrants directly to the Mississippi River which is only a short distance to their wintering grounds. They leave Texas in time to be back in Canada by the first day of May each year in order to keep their insurance. They stay in Canada during the summer and return to the Gulf just before winter. This is a yearly routine and their numbers are comparable to the vast Wildebeest migrations of Africa. During late fall, they pack up and move to the coast, traveling the Natchez Trace Parkway and spending one night free at the Meriwether Lewis Campground. When spring arrives they begin the long trek back to Canada to satisfy the six month in country residency requirement and again use the free facilities at Meriwether Lewis. They travel in very large numbers, all driving rigs that basically are spacious enough to use as full time living quarters for half the year. In other words, they aren't towing pop-ups. Common sense should dictate that folks who can afford to drive a quarter million dollar RV should be able to afford a twenty dollar campground fee, but what would I know about that?

The National Park Service does not accept reservations at Meriwether Lewis, so obtaining a campsite is on a first come, first serve basis. Logic dictates that the Canadians will not arrive early in the morning because they drive all day. So, locals will go very early on Friday to assure themselves a spot for the weekend. In our case, we were camping with another retired couple and leaving early was not a problem. However, another couple in our small group both had full time jobs and could not leave until after work. To insure our friends a site close to us, we were determined to save them a campsite. This is generally not a problem because the campground is rarely full: except when the Canadians arrive. A campsite must show signs of being occupied so I took a small tent and set it up on the site adjacent to the one we were using. I also placed a folding chair in front of the tent and spent part of the day sitting in the chair reading. This plan had been suggested by the fellow who was serving, along with his wife, as campground hosts. They had been there for several weeks and knew all too well what would happen when the caravan of Canadians arrived later in the day. He said he would try to cover for me because he was tired of the local folks coming in after work and not getting a site. No matter what he did, the ultimate decision would be up to the park rangers to determine if I was illegally holding a site. As the afternoon wore on, the available sites were quickly being taken. As I recall there are thirty-one sites at Meriwether. Our friends had one, we had one, our tent was on one and about two other local campers had managed to secure a place before the floodgates opened and the snowbirds arrived.

What transpired that late afternoon in a small rustic campground in southern Tennessee could possibly have set back the relationship between the United States and Canada several hundred years. The battle between the snowbirds and the locals raged throughout the afternoon and into the night. The strategy of the locals was to simply hold on to the territory already in our possession and not give up. We knew the invaders would pull out early the next day and be on their way to the next staging area. With the exception of the couple from Montreal, who were very gracious, the rest were mostly rude and arrogant. As a matter of fact, the folks from Montreal spoke disparagingly of their countrymen. They seemed to have some kind of a grudge against the folks from Quebec. Maybe it had something to do with the independence movement in Quebec to secede from Canada and form their own government. While traveling in the South, they should ask some folks how that idea worked out for us. The travelers from Quebec spoke only French in our presence and we were certain some of the words they used were not very complimentary to Americans. Our friends from Montreal knew very well what they were saying and frequently translated their profanities into English. Some of their words needed little translation. As a matter of fact, I have seen children act more courteous while squabbling over a toy.

There is an old saying that goes something like this: "For the want of a nail the shoe was lost. For the want of a shoe the horse was lost. For the want of a horse the rider was lost. For the want of a rider the battle was lost. For the want of a victory the nation was lost." In our case, the nail was a park ranger who just happened to hail from nearby Hohenwald, Tennessee. His parents frequently faced the same situation we were in while camping at Meriwether and he understood the overwhelming force tactics used by the Canadians. It was our good fortune he was the only ranger on duty that day and was always out on patrol when summoned by the invaders to force us to give up the prized spot. The Canadians circled the campground like the Mexicans at the Alamo. If looks could kill we wouldn't have lasted five minutes. The numbers were on their side but they couldn't get the pesky Americans to surrender. Their last ditch effort failed when our friends finally arrived to claim the site while the Canadian delegation was out searching for the ranger to settle the dispute. They arrived with him in tow and by that time, our friends had already set up their camper. His decision equaled any every made by a judge and it was very simple. He didn't see what the argument was all about because the site was occupied and he wasn't about to throw good Americans out just so people speaking some kind of foreign language would be able to park next to some other folks who spoke the same language. He didn't exactly use those words but we knew where he was coming from, so to speak. Some might call his attitude xenophobic, but we called him a good ole boy from Tennessee. The next morning the enemy had vacated the battle field and the battle of the snowbirds was over, at least for six months.

Singular acts of kindness and diplomacy have been known to change minds and avert wars throughout the history of the civilized world. Since that fateful day in a rustic campground, my attitude toward Tennesseans has changed dramatically. Quite possibly, I have been wrong about a host of other things in my life.

Jackie Hastings

Dogs We Have Known

It is reported that Americans spend billions of dollars a year on their pets, with about forty-five million dollars of this amount being spent on dogs. These numbers have not been broken down into categories but it would be reasonable to believe that most of this money goes toward feed for the critters. Probably the next highest expenditure would be in the area of health care. Our daughter claims it is much more expensive to have pets than children because a trip to the vet requires immediate cash up front while most children are covered by some type insurance. She speaks from experience because her rather large menagerie seems to be a magnet for pet ills and disasters. Margo and I also know this is true because we have spent large sums of money on some of our dogs who were very sick. Our pets have made it a policy to forego mundane illness and instead opt for those rare, hard to treat maladies that send the vet to the computer for research and then to the Mercedes dealer. I suppose feeding and caring for sick animals is one sign of a society which has advanced several steps beyond living in a cave.

Apparently, food and health care do not represent the entire amount people are willing to spend on their pets. It has come to my attention that some folks purchase presents for their pets and one, if he or she so desired, can also purchase clothing designed especially for their furry loved ones. People take them to pet counselors when they appear to be depressed and push them around the neighborhood in fancy strollers as if they were infants. Needless to say, times have certainly changed over the years. When I was a kid, we always had dogs around the place. Their chief function was to bark when strangers arrived on the front porch and to eat the table scraps dumped off the back porch. However, it was not safe for a dog to lurk around the back porch for long periods of time because it could easily find itself in the direct path of hot water thrown out the back door. Thus the phrase, "run like a scalded dog," was something everyone understood. The welfare of dogs and cats was not a major priority at our house because there were other, more pressing problems. In hindsight, I suppose the poor critters often went hungry at our house because my mother had to cook for so many kids and relatives most of our table scraps would fit in a small Bruton snuff can. Needless to say, my community was not aware of pet clothing or presents of any kind. There was one officer on the local police force who drove around and seemed to be on the lookout for stray dogs, especially during the summer. Rabies was a very scary reality back then and all of us were terrified of being bitten by a "mad" dog. If anyone suspected a dog of acting in a strange manner, the officer would simply shoot the critter on sight. It was perhaps a twisted version of the shoot now and ask questions later policy, except the dog was rarely in any kind of shape to answer any questions. Most dogs have life a lot easier nowadays.

There is no doubt that large amounts of cash are also spent on cats, hamsters, goldfish, chickens, ferrets and snakes but few will admit it. There is currently a hamster buried in our backyard with a nice stone marking its final resting place. This little critter was a pet of our grandson when they lived near Cincinnati. As they were preparing to return to Alabama to live, the hamster suddenly passed away. The rumor was that it ate a plastic straw which apparently will not pass through the intestinal tract of a hamster. Thank goodness the little varmint died without fanfare or I am sure the memory of a huge vet bill would be his only legacy. Rather than abandon his remains in a strange, foreign land, his little corpse made the trip south in a shoe box packed in the back of their car. After the funeral entourage arrived at our house, it was given a proper burial in God's country as we stood solemnly around his grave.

When our children were small, we had several near misses with their goldfish but the fish always mysteriously disappeared down the toilet before anyone thought of consulting a vet. Besides, no school of veterinary medicine would take valuable instruction time to teach students how to provide medical care for a goldfish. Therefore, any diagnosis they might make is simply guesswork on their part. I can guess without having to foot an enormous bill.

Cats have quite a fan base but they were rarely noticed at our house while we were growing up. Neither of our parents cared for cats and neither would have ever allowed an animal to live indoors. After all, they did have seven children in and out of the house that had to be fed and that was quite enough. One of my older brothers married a woman who kept cats inside and outside their house for over fifty years of marriage. He was far from a cat lover and I can only assume he must have loved his wife dearly and the presence of so many cats was a price he was willing to pay. He laughingly told me one day that his wife had recently complained about his habit of keeping a loaded pistol near his bed and she wondered why it was necessary for him to do so. His response was to the effect that just in case she died before he did, he wouldn't have to take the time to load the weapon before he could begin shooting cats. Others probably thought he was only kidding but his brothers knew better. Cat lovers will not understand this sentiment but it is more prevalent than they realize. As a matter of fact, I know some very good preachers who do not like cats.

Dogs have been a part of my life since childhood, and I can honestly say they, for the most part, seem to like me. However, as a boy, my brother and I had a paper route and we encountered several biting dogs on a daily basis. Every dog should be allowed one free bite. After that, it has earned a reputation as a biting dog and should be avoided if possible. We did not take it personally that some dogs wanted to bite us and considered it to be an occupational hazard. This is probably also true of mail carriers and meter readers because of their many negative experiences with dogs that bite. Two of my older brothers worked at both these jobs, and, amazingly enough, seemed to carry no grudges. Anyhow, both could hold an audience spell-bound by relating horror stories of these encounters. I do believe if pepper spray had been available back then, it would have been a good investment. Our daddy would not allow us to carry a pistol.

Some folks have even gone so far as to claim pets as exemptions on their tax returns. Apparently, some tax cheating felons are also pet owners. Many citizens of New Orleans refused to evacuate their homes as hurricane Katrina barreled down on them because they would not leave their pets behind. Undoubtedly, many of these folks were among those killed by the storm. As a result of this disaster, communities now include evacuation of pets as part of their preparedness plan. I pity the poor evacuee left behind in the path of a deadly hurricane because the last bus leaving town is already loaded with dogs and cats and there is no more room.

Our family has been blessed to have owned many wonderful dogs as pets over many years. The funny thing is that virtually all of them just sort of fell into our lives without us even looking for a pet. One of the perks of being a parent is that your grown children are always willing to leave you with anything which is a burden for them to take care of, or even find a place to store, when they move out. This includes far more than just pets. It also involves wedding gifts they have never used, old furniture, high school yearbooks, and virtually everything else they have ever owned. Our upstairs attic looks like an overstuffed storage locker.

In all fairness, not all of our pets have been inherited from our children. Some were born on our place, others just showed up uninvited, and, believe it or not, we actually paid good money for one or two. There was one dog we called Junior. It just so happened he was born on our place during the time we were raising feeder pigs to supplement my meager teacher's income. Junior apparently developed an identity problem as a result of spending too much time with the pigs since we were gone during most of the day, either at work or at school. Maybe it was the lack of a positive human role model to bond with but Junior seemed to have a definite preference for swine. It was

128

rather unsettling at first to realize that man's best friend had actually taken up with a bunch of pigs over our loving family. It was not an unusual sight for us to come home and see our dog Junior out in the pasture just hanging out with half a dozen large hogs. Several of our neighbors also noticed our dog's rather strange behavior and questioned Junior's mental stability. The dog seemed to look upon us as his second family and only came to the house to eat his meals, which was even more disturbing. During the time Junior lived at our house, an incident occurred which made me wonder if dogs can actually become deranged to the point that they try to end their own life. I bring this up only because Junior may have actually tried to hang himself. Junior was born at our place and was neutered as a pup. This resulted in him not having a love life of any kind and he did pal around almost exclusively with pigs. These two factors alone could result in severe depression. None of our dogs have been well-travelled and Junior was no exception. The only time he left home was when we took him to the vet for his annual rabies shot and check-up. Thankfully, at the time, we knew nothing of swine flu. On these trips he rode in the back of my pickup which was the usual mode of transportation for dogs at that time. Junior had an odd look in his eye, if you know what I mean, and could not be trusted not to bail out of my truck on a whim. As a result, he was always tethered with a short rope to a cinder block which was supposed to serve as sort of an anchor. On one particular trip, we had left the vet's office and I stopped to get the mail at the road before proceeding up our rather long driveway. Much to my surprise, I discovered that Junior was hanging over the side of the truck bed with his toes barely touching the ground and the rope still secured to the block. Unfortunately, it was also still around his neck. The scene was not unlike a botched hanging in a low budget western movie. He was sort of bouncing up and down like he was on a pogo stick and getting in a little air on the up kick. Obviously, my concern that he might attempt to jump out was well-founded. There was no way of knowing when the ill-fated leap occurred but he was alive and still kicking. Did his rather lackluster life cause him to attempt suicide or was he just that dumb? If it was suicide, at what point did he realize he had made a big mistake and began the long run on his toes? On future trips, he was allowed to ride in the cab of my truck which seemed to please him greatly. My reputation with my neighbors was not real keen most of the time. To be seen dragging my dog behind my truck with a noose around his neck would only have made it much worse. Years later my friend Junior died of old age and is buried in a beautiful spot on a hillside overlooking Cypress Creek.

The only dog which did not wind up at our house by accident was an Australian Shepard named Dolly. We bought her as a puppy for our children in order to teach them the responsibility of owning a pet. Dolly was raised in the house, contrary to everything

Margo and I had espoused over the years, and seemingly thought she was a human. Rocking her to sleep at night may have added to this misunderstanding. She was with us for many years and I am convinced would have attacked a grizzly bear to protect any of her family.

A Golden Retriever named Sam, inherited from our son, spent many years with us. While living near Birmingham, Sam had the reputation as an escape artist. Our son was unable to make his back yard fence secure enough to hold Samson, his legal name. Sam was able to go over the fence, under the fence or through the fence. He only wanted to escape and was not picky about the method. They should have named him Houdini. Complaining neighbors forced a decision on his future and we agreed to let Sam live at our house instead of being carted away to the shelter. Living in the country without the hindrance of a fence suited Sam perfectly and he became a gem of a pet before finally passing on from a variety of illnesses. There was never a kinder, sweeter dog on the face of this earth than our friend, Sam.

The relationship between dogs, however, is not something that is generally talked about. A few years ago, I witnessed an amazing scene that proved to me that dogs have strong feelings and can sense when something bad is happening. Our dogs, Roscoe and Ned, had been with us for many years. Roscoe, a huge, black Lab, was also inherited from our son. Before coming to us, he was confined to a fenced-in back yard all of his life. Our son had him for a couple of years before his job forced him to relocate. If a dog ever yearned for freedom, it was Roscoe. The fence which confined him to our son's back yard was about five feet tall and made of solid wood. In order to see the world outside the fence, Roscoe would bounce up and down like a jumping jack. Every leap brought him a micro-second's view of his small world as his head briefly cleared the top of the fence. If only Roscoe could have talked and had any knowledge of American history, he would have surely been an admirer of Patrick Henry. Of course, we all know from our studies in school he was the American patriot who gave us the immortal words, "give me liberty or give me death," as he implored his fellow colonists not to meekly accept the shackles which bound them to the British. Confinement did not suit Roscoe one little bit.

We try to do as much for our children as we can so we agreed to keep Roscoe at our house in the country. We live in a very rural area surrounded by hundreds of acres of woods, open land and creeks. Fearing Roscoe would get lost; I decided to keep him chained for a few days until he became acclimated to his new home. He had absolutely no previous experience finding his way around in a strange place as he had not been outside a fence his entire life. The restraint seemed to be bothering him, so I decided to release him earlier than I had intended. He started running as soon as the chain came off and ran, to my knowledge, for several days. We thought he was running away to return to his former home and had seen the last of him. Apparently, he didn't want to leave, he just wanted to be able to run for the first time in his life without a fence to make him stop, sort of like an old cowboy riding the open range. He would pass through the yard occasionally and disappear into the woods. No amount of calling him had any effect. He just kept on running. From a distance he could be seen running through the creek bottom and splashing across the creek. After about three days, he came back to the house, plopped down on the back deck and made himself at home. He acted like he had been there forever. It was obvious he loved his new found freedom. Being a Lab, he took great delight in all the water around our place. The pond and creek became his playground.

Roscoe poses proudly in front of his favorite domain, our fish pond.

Although he looked ferocious, he was nothing but a gentle giant but we did not make that fact common knowledge. Roscoe weighed well over a hundred pounds and his ferocious bark was very intimidating to strangers. The Federal Express and UPS people tossed a dog biscuit out the door and soon Roscoe began trying to climb into the truck to fetch his treat. Just the sight of this huge, black dog sent many visitors fleeing down the driveway before we had a chance to discover their intentions.

Ned, on the other hand, was born on our place. He was the offspring of a dropped off female that just wandered up and never left. His father was a complete stranger, sort of a roving vagabond, who stayed only a few days lurking around the edge of the woods bordering our yard. The scoundrel lingered only long enough to leave us with a litter of pups. Thankfully, we were successful in giving most of them to friends. One pup was extremely shy and would not allow anyone to touch him so he was never adopted. If Sigmund Freud had been able to analyze the pup, he would probably have concluded his poor self-concept was somehow caused by issues related to his mother but we will never know. Instead of analyzing poor Ned, we just accepted the fact that he did not cater to strangers. Not catering to strangers is a poor person's way to describe something a psychiatrist would call anthrophobia, which is an irrational fear of people. Actually, in this respect, Ned simply took on a character quirk that has apparently plagued me for many years. As a boy I was prone to climb a tree or hide in the barn when we had company at our house. This aberrant behavior never reached the level of a full-fledged phobia but it has left a significant gap in my social skills. My wife might even say that I have yet to outgrow this rather strange behavior but, she doesn't complain because it keeps me out of the house. Since I am too old to climb trees, I just go to my workshop and hang out.

In spite of his many short-comings, we decided to keep the pup and eventually began calling him Ned simply because the name seemed to fit. Ned never outgrew his reclusive ways. When people visited, Ned would disappear and not return until they were gone. Meanwhile, Roscoe would rush out to meet them, convinced they had come to our house solely for the purpose of visiting him. The only danger he presented to anyone was a death brought about by excessive licking. Ned refused to eat if being watched, while Roscoe was gobbling up everything in sight. The pair could be described as polar opposites. When called to the house, Roscoe would come running, probably expecting a giant steak. On the other hand Ned could be seen slinking away, always expecting the worst. Gauging by his reaction, one would have thought we water-boarded him on a regular basis. Roscoe was a slobbering optimist while his friend Ned was a pessimist with maybe a touch of paranoia. But, they were great pets and got along nicely.

After living with us for several years, Roscoe became extremely sick. The vet diagnosed his illness as spore borne and contracted by his favorite activity, digging. The sickness was usually fatal but we refused to give him up without a fight. We became part of the statistic that about 70% of pet owners are willing to spend any amount to save a beloved pet. After spending days at the vet undergoing treatment, he made a miraculous, and expensive, recovery. However, the disease cost him the sight in one eye and left him with a lasting arthritic condition. His quality of life was very good for several more years and then began a slow decline. Finally, giving in to the vet's suggestion, we reluctantly agreed to have him put down.

The final trip to the vet's office was something I did not think I could handle emotionally. Thankfully, my wife volunteered for the job because she knew I would break down and cry like a baby. For years, one of Roscoe's favorite things to do was to ride in the back of my truck. It mattered not to him where I was going, he just wanted to come along. I can still see him, facing the wind, with his huge ears flopping wildly. When he was young, he could jump into the truck bed but, after the illness, we had to give him some help. Too heavy to lift, I always backed up to a wall and allowed him to walk into the bed. I loaded Roscoe for the last time and watched as my wife drove away. Then, an amazing thing happened. Ned, who had just stood nearby and watched what was going on, began howling and following after the truck as it disappeared down our driveway. His presence had gone unnoticed in the emotion of the moment and the noise startled me. The sound was not a bark, not a yip, but a long, sorrowful howl. Ned continued on, and on, and on for a long time, even after the truck had disappeared. It was as though Ned was aware that his friend was leaving and would not return. Some would probably scoff at the idea that Ned knew what was happening and explain it another way. Maybe he could sense the sorrow that I felt, I don't know. The loss of his friend was evident by his behavior because he acted like a different dog for weeks to come. He became even more reclusive and lived only a few more months until he died.

It is impossible for a human to try to explain, much less, understand, what emotions an animal might be experiencing. I have enough trouble understanding some of my own feelings and certainly have no clue as to what might be going through the head of animals. People who have studied the question of whether or not animals experience emotions offer a mix bag of results. I have been around animals of all kinds all my life and I know, without a doubt, they do express emotions in an observable manner. Obviously, they become attached to each other just as we become attached to them. All I know is that I saw what I saw.

The Lord in all His wisdom gave us pets, especially dogs, to provide a lot of things: companionship being among the most valuable. People are able to bond with their pets in a manner which many folks do not understand. Saying good-bye to a loyal friend is one of the most painful and emotional experiences a pet owner can ever have. Some folks who have gone through the loss of a pet refuse to ever own another one. I hesitate to use the word, "own," because they own us more than we own them. I have often wondered if it was worth the pain but the memories always provide an immediate answer.

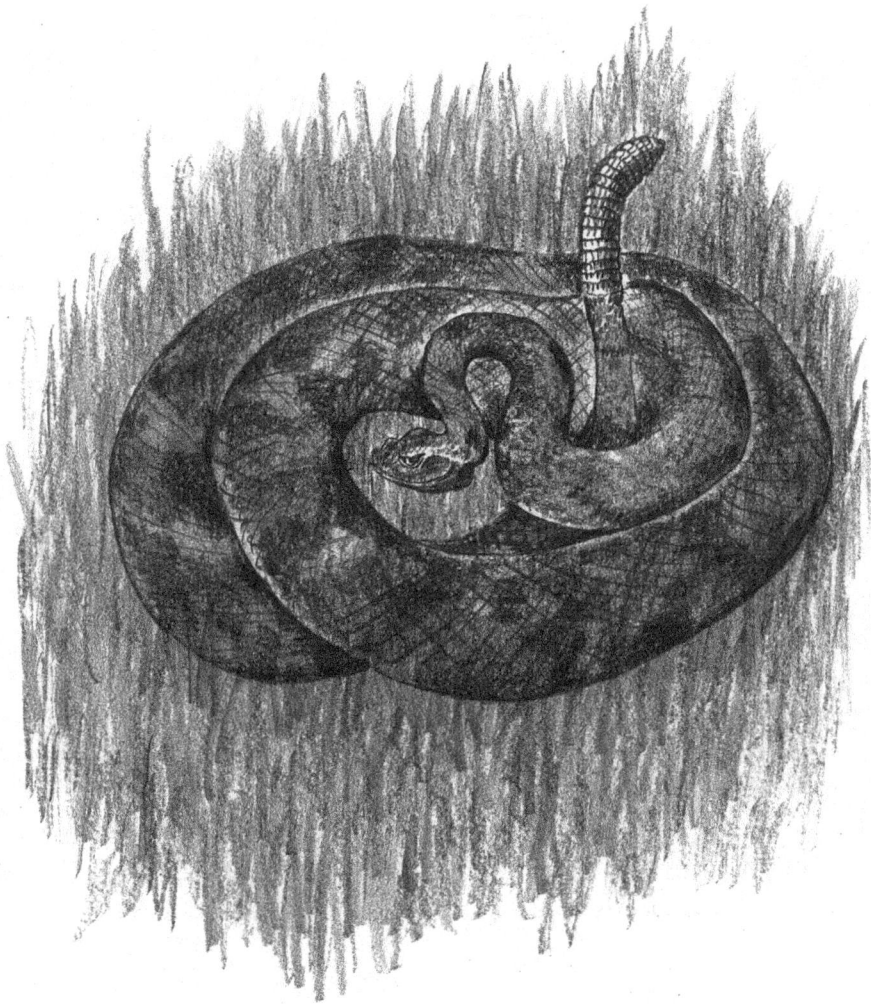

Snake Stories

It seems that snakes have been the nemesis of man since the Garden of Eden when Satan himself, some believe in the form of a snake, told the first of millions of lies and deceived Eve into taking a bite of the forbidden fruit. Mention the word snake in and around some folks and it's like yelling "theatre" in a crowded fire. I may have that backward but the meaning should be obvious. Some folks have a fear of snakes that defies all logic. Even when it is behind glass or twenty yards away, they still cannot handle the situation. There is not a hoe handle in the world long enough to convince my wife she could safely chop off the head of a snake without being bitten. According to her, a snake can strike the length of a football field with the accuracy of a sniper. My daddy would have fought a grizzly bear with a fly swatter but show him a green snake and he would have trampled girl scouts and old ladies in an attempt to put distance between him and the perfectly harmless critter.

I must confess to being a practical joker since I can remember and my dad was often a victim when it came to snake jokes. He was such an easy mark that I couldn't help myself. I kept a long rubber snake around and would frequently place it on a shelf about head high in his shop or in the feed barrel where I knew he would see it. My favorite was the feed barrel because he was sort of bent over and his head was in a confined space which accentuated the panic. Daddy was not a man prone to hysterics, except when confronted face-to-face with a snake, real or rubber. I just had to remember to observe the situation from a distance because it was not wise to get within arm's reach of him until he quieted down a bit. This was a time in my life when my vocabulary grew immensely, although many of the new words could not be used in polite company.

To me, snakes have never been the scary creatures they are to other folks. It is not the snake itself but the surprise that affects most folks. I don't love snakes and I would not want one for a pet or to keep one in my house but they don't terrify me as long as I can see it. As a matter of fact, people who keep snakes in their house should be institutionalized. My working theory is that the snake you don't see is the one that gets you. I have had several encounters with snakes and have not yet been scarred for life or driven into counseling. This statement may be debatable because some of my friends have suggested counseling would not be a bad idea for a variety of reasons not necessarily related to snakes.

Those who choose to live in rural areas pretty much accept the presence of snakes as a way of life. Not only is there plenty of cover for snakes but oftentimes rural dwellers actually attract snakes, and other predators, by cultivating a food source for them at their doorstep. A prime example is the presence of chickens, especially laying hens. Chickens attract predators by the score: those that walk, those that fly and, yes, those that crawl. Colonel Sanders wasn't the first to discover that chickens make a pretty tasty meal. Over the years, my chickens have attracted hawks, owls, coyotes, fox, possums, bobcats, raccoons and, inevitably, snakes. My suspicions about midnight visits to the chicken house by my neighbors have not yet been proven.

Not only do snakes prey on the chicken, but eggs are also a delicacy for these critters. Speaking of which, one of our favorite dogs of all time was an egg sucker. She was the prettiest little Border Collie you could imagine and loved us fiercely after we rescued her from a life of being tied to a stake in someone's yard. She wouldn't bother a chicken at all but she dearly loved to get into the hen house and suck the inside of an egg out of a tiny hole she chewed in the shell. The term, "sorry as an egg-sucking dog," never gained a lot of traction at our house because we thought a whole lot of the dog. Our attitude was, what the heck, nobody's perfect. If some of the human species could limit all their bad traits to just being an egg sucker it would be a better world and the egg market would flourish.

Sometime during the 1970's, the decade is easy to remember because I was wearing bell-bottom jeans, I was hoeing our garden and from the nearby barn I could hear one of my hens squawking up a storm. One of the hens had hatched off a bunch of chicks and it sounded like something was after one of them. I rushed to the barn and there, right smack in the middle of the hall, was a huge chicken snake with a chick in its mouth. The hen was pecking furiously at it and raising quite a ruckus. There was no time to waste because once the snake cleared the hallway it would be long gone and I would be out one baby chick and most of the others over a period of time. Without thinking, I rushed over and stepped on the snake, right behind his head. Now, chicken snakes grow to be very large and this was one of the larger ones.

I made mention earlier of wearing bell-bottom jeans at the time. As impossible as it may seem, there may actually be people who are not familiar with that particular piece of apparel. They look like regular slim leg jeans from about the knee up. Below the knee, they begin to flare out and get wider as they approach the foot and sort of resemble a bell. At that time of my life bell-bottom pants were a sign of being chic and the man who wore them, along with a purple Nehru jacket, was obviously a man of style and class. Also, the centerpiece of my ward robe during those days was a spiffy green leisure suit with bell bottom jeans. Today, a man similarly attired would be pitied and ignored by polite society. We all know that change happens whether we like it or not.

Well anyway, this snake was in excess of four feet and I had about six inches on the front end penned to the ground with my foot. The remaining four feet or so found the extremely large opening in the bottom of my pants leg and up my leg went the tail end of the snake. It wrapped itself around my leg, from my knee down and its tail was thrashing wildly against my leg.

People may define a predicament in many different ways I suppose, depending on one's personality and temperament. One dictionary defines predicament as, "a difficult situation in which there is no easy escape." This definition just about hit the nail on the head. No matter how one chooses to describe the situation, it was definitely a dire one. My first impulse was to jump as high as I could but there was a distinct possibility the rest of that snake would follow the tail and find its way up my britches leg. This could easily be described as finding oneself in a "pickle."

A chicken snake is a member of the constrictor family which kills its prey by slowly wrapping around it and the coils constrict, eventually crushing and killing the animal in its grasp. Because it was a constrictor, the portion of the snake inside my pants leg wrapped around my bare leg and began squeezing. A snake just less than five feet in length is no threat to a human and there was no danger to me whatsoever, except maybe heart failure. However, the feel of that snake wrapped around my bare leg and squeezing was one I do not wish to experience anytime in the future.

There were various objects on either side of the hall which could be used as a weapon and I would have killed the snake if possible. However, I was in the middle of the hallway and could not reach either side. Other than a shotgun, a hoe is about the best snake fighting weapon known to man, but I had left my hoe in the garden. When the panic subsided, I realized the snake was no threat and the baby chick was already dead. There was enough of its body sticking out from under my foot to get a firm grip so I reached down and grabbed the snake just behind its head. At that point I removed my foot and held it out to look at it. It was very close to five feet and suddenly I was struck by a marvelous idea.

I had the perfect object in my hand to play a great trick on Margo, my beloved wife. As I said earlier, she has a terror of snakes that bordered on being irrational.

Holding my new found toy, I went to the house and lay on the ground outside the front door. With the snake wrapped around my neck and shoulders and me gripping it behind the head, my screams of terror brought her running to my rescue. That is, until she saw the snake. She came to a screeching halt, shut the door and I could hear her locking it from the inside. No amount of pleading on my part would bring her back to the door. My practical joke was funny for about five seconds, until I realized she was perfectly willing to turn her idiot of a husband over to the snake. This strange turn of events provided me plenty of opportunity to wonder, what if?

That question was at least partially answered a few years later after we built a new house in a very rural area. One of my favorite warm weather things to do is to sit on the front porch at night and just listen to all the night sounds. The frogs are making a ruckus in the pond and creek while the tree frogs are doing their thing. An occasional conversation between two or three owls on opposite sides of our yard and the whip-poor-wills calling to each other combine to make a sound that puts the greatest orchestra to shame, at least to my way of looking at things. Many a night I have spent hours in the porch swing marveling at what God has created and how He had blessed me with the privilege of living in the midst of it all. Our front porch has two swings and the one I usually sat in was to the left of the front door. To say it gets really dark at our house is an understatement. Since our son left home, he has basically been a city slicker. He has remarked on more than one occasion that it gets darker at our house than anywhere in the world.

It never failed that when I opened the door to go out onto the extremely dark porch, Margo would say, "You had better turn that porch light on and check for snakes." As I said earlier, she evidently spent a lot of time thinking about snakes. Her level of vigilance was always extremely high. Instead of ignoring her on this particular night, I took her advice and switched on the light. As luck would have it, lying stretched out in the direct path between the door and the swing was a two-foot long copperhead. This was not good. A chicken snake or a green snake on the front porch is not bad but a copperhead presents a totally different problem.

Of all the poisonous snakes in our area, the copperhead, the rattlesnake and the cottonmouth, I fear the copperhead the most. They strike without warning. A rattler normally gives a warning before it strikes. Anytime I am around a body of water, I keep a sharp lookout for cottonmouths but I have never seen one any distance from water.

My normal path to the swing would have taken me directly across the snake. Obviously, I had to kill the critter before it escaped into the night. The snake began a slow crawl toward the edge of the porch and the only weapon I saw close by was a rocking chair. My plan was to rock the chair forward until it penned the snake to the floor and, in the meantime, call for help. My plan was apparently poorly thought out and did not work well in any respect. The snake became very agitated as I tried to pen it and came in my direction very aggressively. Margo sauntered to the door and told me my shouting was spoiling her nap. I very politely asked her to bring me something that would kill the snake which by now was in full attack mode. The use of the word snake caused her to spring into action. She immediately shut the door and locked it from the inside. Where had I seen her do that before?

In my state of near panic, it was very troubling to hear the door being locked. Was she trying to keep me or the snake out of the house? Had I been wrestling a bear on the front porch, locking the door may have been somewhat logical since a bear might fumble around and unknowingly open an unlocked door. However, I seriously doubt a snake could perform such a feat because everyone knows that snakes do not have a thumb. Tree huggers and others of their like have told me at various times that copperheads are not aggressive and will always flee when people approach. Their advice is simply to relocate the snake to another location. They would probably offer the same advice about a rabid dog. Do not accept that theory as an absolute fact and always seek a second opinion. In other words, call me if you want to get the real truth of the matter. This snake attacked me on my front porch. My sole intention was to separate it from its head and relocation was not going to happen. If this snake managed to escape, Margo would be the one relocating.

My strategic withdrawal continued, some might refer to it as a retreat, across the porch, keeping the rocking chair between me and the snake. At last, the front door opened and Margo handed me a broom and said, as she shut and locked the door, "That is all I can find." I discovered almost immediately that it is impossible to kill an enraged copperhead with a broom. I continued to plead for something with sharp metal on the end.

The next time the door opened, a pitch fork was tossed out the door before it was once again closed and locked. My first thought was to wonder why she had a pitch fork in the house. We had a pitch fork but it was always kept in the barn. There was absolutely no way she would go to the barn in the dark because, as she told me many times, "I might run across a snake." A pitch fork does have metal on the end in the form of three tines.

140

However, these tines are about four inches apart and one would have to sort of spear the snake on a tine as it was charging across the porch and this was very difficult to do holding a rocking chair in one hand and constantly retreating, or rather, withdrawing.

There are times in life when we must learn to make do with what we have at hand. This is a life lesson and is worth repeating to children until they are sick of hearing it. That night, alone on my front porch staring down a copperhead intent on sinking its fangs into my quivering flesh, I discovered something most people would never dream to be possible: one can kill a snake with a rocking chair if the appropriate level of desperation is reached. The reptile was dispatched, after what seemed to be an eternity, and its skin still adorns the wall of my workshop door. As a matter of fact, two copperhead skins are tacked side by side on this door. As you may have guessed, this story has another chapter.

About a week later, having taken to heart my wife's advice to switch on the porch light before going out on the front porch after dark, I harkened back to my days in elementary school and looked both ways. Sure enough, this time to the right of the door was another copperhead.

I failed to mention that earlier in my life I spent a short period of time in Boy Scout Troop 55, operating out of Saint James Methodist Church on Sweetwater Avenue in the middle of East Florence. Since I was not able to advance beyond the rank of what is known, somewhat derisively I might add, in the Boy Scouts as, Tenderfoot, I dropped out in order to seek other opportunities, as a disgraced politician might say today. There is no doubt that advancement to a loftier rank would have been in my future had it not been for all those knots that were required in order to be promoted. I could tie a square knot which seemed sufficient to me but the Boy Scout manual insisted on knots that not even a sailor could tie on a sailing schooner in the middle of the Pacific. Be that as it may, one thing I did retain from this brief experience was the Boy Scout motto, "Be Prepared." This time I was prepared in the form of a hoe kept in a permanent location on the back porch.

My previous experience of using a rocking chair as a weapon was not for naught and keeping a hoe within reach was a lesson well learned. There is a difference between being dumb and stupid. This snake was as good as dead. All that was necessary was for me to keep my eye on the rascal while Margo fetched the hoe. It was at this extremely unfortunate time that my reputation as a practical joker caught up with me. My frantic calls of "snake, snake" were unheeded. Apparently, Margo thought I was crying wolf and refused to take the bait. The snake, alarmed by all the shouting, began to slither toward the edge of the porch. If it escaped we would be faced with the prospect of living in fear of encountering another copperhead at any time on the porch.

Seeing no other recourse, I made for the rocking chair and barely managed to pen the snake. Just as before, his attention was focused on me instead of escaping. Once again I found myself the victim of a snake attack. Utilizing my experience with the rocking chair, I was much more adept at fending off his strikes. The air reeked of the musky smell of snake venom. Finally, alarmed by all the commotion on the porch, Margo came to the door to check out the situation. At the sight of the snake, her gazelle like reflexes kicked in as she slammed and locked the door. My childhood idol, Yogi Berra, would say of this situation, "It was déjà vu all over again." But this time, instead of a broom, she returned and handed me the hoe out the door and the snake soon lost its head. The skin became a reminder that lightning can strike twice in the same place.

It might be hard to imagine anything worse than having a snake on the front porch but, believe me, it is far worse to have one inside your living quarters. This very nightmare occurred a few years later when we were spending a few days during the Fall at Desoto State Park in Northeast Alabama. This is a very beautiful part of the state and very reminiscent of the sights one would see in the Great Smoky Mountains. It is very mountainous and full of fast moving streams, waterfalls, deep gorges and wildlife. It is located in a very isolated area and vehicle traffic is virtually nonexistent.

Margo and I had rented one of the rustic cabins at the park for a few days. Nestled atop a high ridge overlooking a stream, it was a very relaxing environment in which to enjoy nature. That is until the snake fell off the door and smacked right onto the living room floor. We were leaving to go to the lodge restaurant for dinner and as I opened the front door of the cabin, out of the corner of my eye I picked up something falling. Somehow the little snake had managed to crawl up the log wall and found a comfortable spot atop the door where it stretched out and, as far as it knew, had not a care in the world. When the door was abruptly pulled open it just tumbled off the door onto the floor and the world around it went haywire.

Before I could determine exactly what had happened, some primordial instinct apparently alerted my wife to the presence of a snake and she thundered past me onto the relative safety of the screened in front porch of the cabin. Thank goodness the cabins were spaced quite a distance a part, otherwise, the whooping and yelping would have convinced them we were under attack from the long gone Cherokees who inhabited the region many years ago. The cause of the ruckus was a green snake about sixteen inches

142

long and totally harmless, except maybe causing Margo to suffer a massive coronary. There was no need to panic but I did feel a need to remove the snake from the inside of the cabin before it slithered under a couch or chair and disappeared.

Had the unthinkable occurred, our stay atop the mountain would have come to an abrupt halt. As a matter of fact, we would have just abandoned our clothes and any other items we had taken inside the cabin. There was absolutely no way Margo would have gone back inside to retrieve any of our belongings. Our only option would have been to return home with only the clothes on our back. There was no way to completely sanitize a piece of luggage which had been anywhere near a snake. With this in mind, I attempted to sort of kick the snake out the already open door. Keep in mind my wife was on the porch and it was not nearly large enough for both of them. My kick was true and accurate and as the snake became airborne and sailed through the door Margo retreated even further into the yard, all the while railing at me to get rid of the snake. Luckily I was able to get the snake off the porch and onto the ground where it beat a path to the nearby woods, scared out of its wits.

After taking a while to calm down, Margo was able to eat supper at the lodge restaurant. Unfortunately, the poor lodge manager happened to be wandering around the dining room asking his guests how they were enjoying their stay. Hearing Margo's snake story, which immediately attracted the attention of everyone within earshot, and fearful of sending his guests stampeding down the mountain, he immediately dispatched every maintenance person at his disposal to our little cabin and had it searched high and low for varmints of any kind. The remainder of our stay was very peaceful except for the fact that my wife did not walk but ran through every doorway she encountered. This would not have seemed so odd except I noticed several other women engaging in the same kind of strange behavior. I can only presume that those women not running through doorways were not in the dining room while Margo narrated her terrifying run-in with what surely had to be a cobra on Sand Mountain.

Encountering a harmless snake in the wild is no big deal but running into a real live poisonous critter like a timber rattler can be a totally different experience. Several years back, a friend and I traveled from Tennessee into North Carolina to visit a place called Cataloochee. This extremely remote and isolated high valley in the North Carolina region of the Smoky Mountains is where the National Park Service released elk back into the wild in 2001. Margo and I had visited the area previously but she refused to return. Traveling the high, narrow road over the mountain into the valley was such a terrifying experience she vowed never to go back. My friend and I arrived in the late afternoon hoping to catch a view of the elk as they came down from the surrounding mountainside to graze in the several hundred acre valley floor. While waiting, we noticed what appeared to be a common black snake crossing the trail a few yards away.

Most people react in one of two ways when they see a snake. One group is comprised of folks who have a mortal fear of snakes and they go screaming in the opposite direction. The other group is made up of folks who want to approach the snake and prod it along. Both my friend and I just happened to be members of the prodding group. However, what appeared to be a black snake turned out to be a rather large timber rattler. We could easily determine that because it had about eight rattles on its tail. The almost black coloration was confusing until I was told later that it could have been about ready to shed the skin. After taking a few pictures, the snake slithered on out of sight and we lost track of it. Some other folks came along and we warned them of its presence. However, the last fellow to appear wore a Tennessee Volunteer shirt and we just let him go without informing him that a rattlesnake was nearby. Was that really wrong?

In conclusion, I must admit that over the years my wife has grown more tolerant of snakes. She has possibly been the inadvertent beneficiary of a counseling technique called operant conditioning. Very simply put, if someone fears heights for example, exposing that person a little bit at a time to heights will slowly help them overcome their fear. The patient may go from standing on the bottom rung of a ladder to a first floor window and gradually on up to the top floor of a sky scraper without exhibiting overt signs of an unusual and debilitating fear that inhibits everyday life. Margo has been able to at least abide the presence of a snake because of her almost fifty year marriage to me. If she had married someone who lived in a penthouse, she would still be deathly afraid of snakes because she would not have had the exposure I was able to provide her. However, we have always lived in rural areas and snakes are almost a part of daily life in warm weather. I am sure at times she has thought I actually went out of my way to seek out snakes but that is far from the truth. It just happened that way.

As evidence of her improvement in this area let me describe another encounter we had with a snake while hiking in the Smoky Mountains. We were hiking up a very narrow mountain side trail and had almost reached the summit when we rounded a bend and in front of us, right in the middle of the trail, lay a huge timber rattler, already coiled with its rattle buzzing. It heard us coming and was preparing to defend itself if necessary. We stopped about ten feet from it and pondered our options. The Margo of yesteryear would have considered only one option and that would have been to go screaming back down the trail and lock herself in the car. She did suggest that as one alternative but agreed with me that since we were so close to the top of the mountain it would have been a shame to quit before we reached our goal. There was no walking around the snake since the trail was only about three feet wide. To our right the mountain dropped off precipitously and to our left the mountain rose at a very steep angle. She wisely vetoed my suggestion we bypass the snake by climbing above it and clinging to the brush until we could safely come back down to the trail on the other side of the snake. A misstep or a broken limb would have caused us to fall on top on the critter. We were finally able to make it move down the mountain side by patiently tossing small pebbles at it until it became so annoyed it retreated. As it stretched out to crawl away we could see how really large a snake we had encountered face to face and won the standoff. We made it to the top in just a few minutes and were rewarded with a view that was truly awesome.

As I bragged on her remarkable improvement toward snakes, I couldn't help but think she was probably wishing she had married the guy that lived in the penthouse.

Jackie Hastings

Summertime

As we grow older we can be certain of a lot more things than when we were younger. That is not to say we are right more often but we just tend to think we are right and others are wrong. Age tends to bring things more into focus or at least it has for me. Our experiences in life tend to shape our actions and our thinking. This doesn't mean that I am any smarter than at other time of my life but perhaps experience gives us more certainty and certainty about life gives the perception of wisdom, even if it is false. Unfortunately, unless we learn early in life to keep our mouth shut, that perception fades rapidly.

If we think we have whipped this world we are sadly mistaken. This is a rather drastic turnaround from what I believed when I was young. Optimism in a young person is a wonderful trait and I never want to be guilty of trying to take that away from anyone. As a matter of fact, I hope at least a few minutes of my last day will be spent optimistically planning what I will do tomorrow. For the great majority of us, when we die, this world will be pretty much the same as we found it, a continual struggle between good and evil until time is no more. Other than making things right with our Maker, about the only thing we can do with the time we spend on this planet is to do our best to conquer the fear, doubt, and hatred that exists in our own life and hope it is contagious and spreads to others.

It doesn't take a whole lot of wisdom to understand that as we watch the years pass by our remaining years grow fewer in number. Nothing can be done about this because it is the natural progression of the cycle of life. In my own life, there are a lot of things I will miss from my younger days and, consequently, a number of things which I will not miss. However, summertime is one part of my young life I look back on with a great deal of nostalgia.

Summer to an adult means something entirely different than summer to a twelve year old boy. At this time of my life summer is the time of the year I like to spend resting on the porch reading a good book and drinking ice tea to escape the heat of the day. As a boy, summer was a time of great adventure and a degree of independence not known during the long, tortuous school year. It would be great to anticipate those wonderful days in the same manner as I did then. Those days will never return because too many doors have opened and closed since that time of my life.

I do not know how people in other places spend their summers and, consequently, cannot speak with any authority on that subject. However, being a child of the South, I can speak with a degree of certainty about how those of my generation, the so-called Baby Boomers, spent those special days of their lives. The only really bad thing about summers is that they are separated by approximately nine months of agony called the school year. I can well remember sprinting out the front door and down the hill on which my elementary school stood shouting, along with my heathen friends, "Schools out, schools out, teachers let the mules out." Normally a person would not use the word "heathen" to describe his friends. My mother used this word repeatedly when talking about them and from what little I know about heathens, she hit the nail on the head.

As Baby Boomers we are the children of what is known as the "greatest generation." We have been cussed and discussed as long as I can remember. Depending on the speaker, we have either been a blessing to the nation or the source of many problems. We are either a drain on the Social Security system or the capitalists who ruined the world. Our generation produced the hippie movement and Woodstock and propelled the Beatles into the stratosphere of world-wide fame. We have lived through more wars than most folks and the polio epidemic took many of us to an early grave or to an iron lung. But, if we were anything, we were creative. We were basically born before television, computers, Facebook, and cell phones. Going to the moon was only something we read about in science fiction books. We are not "connected" as some like to think of themselves. A "tweet" was the distinctive sound made by a bird. Any reference to something "going viral" does not send me scampering to my computer but, instead, makes me wonder if the Black Plague has returned. There were no water slides, adult organized and dominated sports, or any of the other myriad of distractions that are now available to the youth of today.

Many people refer to the generation of young people today as an "entitled" generation. They were basically born into a world of ease and comfort and feel they are entitled to nothing but the very best life has to offer. The idea of starting a job at the bottom and working their way to the top is foreign to their very nature. That may or may not be true. Being considerably older, I have no clue what younger folks might be thinking. However, if they do think along those lines, then heaven help them when reality hits home.

Growing up when and where I did, if we had any fun, we had to create it on our own. Adults did not spend their valuable time trying to keep kids occupied with fun activities. Boys my age carried a day's worth of fun in their front pocket; namely marbles,

148

a pocketknife and usually a piece of sewing thread from our mother's sewing box. A gang of boys with a pocket full of marbles and a patch of dirt could spend hours winning and losing their favorite cat-eye. We played either funnsies or keepsies. In funnsies, all your marbles were returned after the match and in keepsies the winner kept his gains. It was highly possible to go home empty handed, especially if you got matched up with a real sharpie. My mother always became terribly distraught when she discovered I had apparently won marbles from another kid. To her, this was gambling, pure and simple. I soon learned not to ever show her my marble stash. This enabled me to stave off many lectures about the condition of my soul and its ultimate destination. It has been decades since I have seen a group of kids playing marbles and that is a shame. Instead of gambling with marbles, they are probably accompanying their parents to Tunica on a regular basis.

Kites were big when I was a boy. The best time for flying kites is always March because this is the month when the wind is most consistent. However, March is an unpredictable time of year and Saturday was not always conducive to kite flying so we also did a lot of kite flying during the summer. A complete kit for assembling a kite could be purchased for about a quarter but sometimes this princely sum was not available. Instead, we just built our own. Some old newspaper, glue from Daddy's shop and some hollow reeds from the creek bank were all the materials necessary to get a project of this nature off the ground, in a manner of speaking. A beautifully assembled kite is of absolutely no value and will not ever fly unless the tail is just right. We used old rags, ripped into strips and tied together for this last, but extremely vital, stage of construction. A kite in mid-flight is beautiful to behold but tragedy can strike quickly. It is not uncommon to launch a kite and never see it again. The chief culprit is a broken string. When this happens the kite just disappears and flies away, probably to land miles away in the backyard of some kid who claims it as his own. Some trees are apparently kite magnets. A very successful flight can turn catastrophic when, for some unknown reason, the kite suddenly begins a fatal nosedive into the top of a kite eating tree. This happened to my kites so frequently that it had to be something other than mere coincidence. A kite lodged in the top of a large tree is a lost cause. I have stood at the base of giant oaks on far too many occasions looking up at my shredded, but once beautiful kite speared by tree branches. Perhaps the lesson a kite flyer learns early is to enjoy blessings while they are with us. A beautiful kite can disappear in the blink of an eye without warning. Life is sort of like that.

A pocketknife was the source of a variety of fun activities. There is just some sort of attraction between a boy and a knife that can't be explained. This love of pocket knives is sometimes carried over into adulthood and there are many men who collect and cherish the knives of their youth. We whittled on sticks, carved our names on trees for posterity's sake, honed our knife throwing skills by constantly clanging the knife off whatever target was at hand and played mumbletypeg. As far as I can tell the game of mumbletypeg is a lost art. The game involved holding your knife in a variety of positions against a part of your body and then flipping it to make it stick up in the ground. If your opponent could not replicate the throw, a point was scored. It was great fun but sometimes resulted in a knife wound to the foot which tended to anger the father of the victim. Sometimes on a really bad day, a kid could lose all his marbles and his pocketknife and arrive home with a puncture wound which probably required a visit to the doctor and a tetanus shot. In addition, he had to face a father angered by the five-dollar doctor bill and the fact that he had sired a stupid son.

Generally, the June bugs showed up just about the same time school let out for the summer. They could normally be found on hedges and other bushes. It was easy to mistake them for a bumble bee and that mistake always resulted in a nasty sting. Some kid in the group always had a cigarette or tobacco in some form and a sloppy wad of tobacco on the sting would take the pain away very quickly. The June bugs provided a barrel of fun, for us, not the bugs. We captured them and tied a length of string to one of their back legs and ran along behind them as they flew around. It was sort of like flying a very small model airplane attached to a wire. We went through a lot of bugs because the string pulled their leg off or they soon became exhausted and fell to the ground. Boys sometimes have a tendency to overdo a good thing.

I never acquired a foot wound from a knife that warranted a trip to the doctor but my angry father had to take me to the doctor for something far worse. Maybe I have already mentioned that boys are prone to do things that turn out to be really stupid in hindsight but, at the time, seem like a perfectly good idea. My cousin and I were engaged in a serious contest to determine which of us could snort a pebble the longest distance. However, the rules are not carved in stone and accuracy can be substituted for distance by mutual agreement. The rules of the contest were very simple: insert a small pebble into either nostril, take in a deep breath through the mouth and exhale violently through the nose. Theoretically, the pebble will exit the nostril, sort of like a cannon ball. This does work and is great fun; however there is one very serious drawback. It is extremely important that while drawing in the deep breath it is done entirely through the mouth. If any portion of this sudden influx of air happens to come in through the nostril containing the pebble, bad things can, and do, happen. The worst is that the pebble is sucked farther up into the nostril and cannot be dislodged no matter how much snorting takes place.

This is bad in itself but it is not by any means the worst part of this self-inflicted ordeal. The worst part for me was the looming certainty that I had to tell my daddy what I had done. He took great pride in attempting to instill in his children the importance of using common sense and my actions frequently ran counter to that policy. Daddy was a fixer with a tool box and a whole shop full of tools at his disposal. I had been his patient many times while he took a splinter out of my finger or a gnat out of my eye. He did not suffer fools gladly and expected stoic acceptance of any pain he might unintentionally inflict while performing the task at hand. Pain is frequently the price we pay for stupid decisions. As the father of seven children, he had a vast amount of experience dealing with self-inflicted injuries. Actually, we often injured each other but never seriously. However, the pebble up the nose stunt was his first and sort of baffled him. Initially, he attempted to extract the pebble using his needle nose pliers but was successful only in making my nose bleed. The entire time the pliers were in my nose he was lecturing me, which was almost as bad as a whipping.

Finally, he could see no other recourse than to take me to the trusted family doctor for professional help. This was totally out of character for him and was extremely alarming for his patient. Daddy made it a practice of having each of his children inoculated with a tetanus shot. It seemed we stepped on an inordinate number of rusty nails and that was about the only reason a doctor might be needed. Visiting a doctor for something other than a shot was a new experience for me. Dr. Cloyd seemed somewhat amused by my predicament and I was fairly certain he and my daddy had some kind of understanding that the upcoming procedure to remove the pebble should be painful enough to teach me a good lesson.

The nurse shined a light up my nose while the doctor used long, pointed metal instruments which successfully removed the small rock but also scared me out of my wits. Although it cost my daddy five dollars, it was a lesson well learned. But my cousin did not learn anything from my harrowing experience. A common trait shared by most people is that we do not learn from our own mistakes or from the mistakes of others.

Several weeks later he was attempting the same feat using a pinto bean as a projectile. Feats not requiring the use of a brain may be a solo act or involve a partner. As with me, he sucked in through the nose with the same result. Moisture in the upper reaches of the nostril caused the bean to swell and created quite a scene at his house. His difficulty breathing was made worse because he kept running through the house screaming at the top of his lungs. We could hear the ruckus from our house but were polite enough not to go snooping around. He eventually collapsed due to a lack of oxygen to his brain. The ambulance attendants had to strap him to the stretcher and take him to the emergency room where the bean was surgically extracted.

The arrival of an ambulance in our neighborhood was always a really big event and the inevitable gawkers soon gathered. His ordeal made my trip to see the family doctor look kind of lame. Needless to say, my daddy took advantage of the situation and used my friend's unfortunate ambulance ride as a teachable moment and seemed overly concerned about how much it cost.

Summer vacation to a twelve year boy in the 1950's is hard to put into words. Nobody in their right mind would hire a kid to do any kind of serious job in those days so we were pretty much left to our own resources. Aside from a few assigned chores, the time was ours to do with as we pretty well pleased. A twelve year boy has the world at his door step. He is not limited by the constraints he experienced when he was younger and always under the watchful eye of a parent. A twelve year old is generally pleasant and has not yet become a wiseass teenager who knows everything and respects nothing. His hormones have not yet started to boil and erupt into an embarrassing case of acne and a vision of the opposite sex that would mortify his mother and make her start looking under his mattress. He can discuss really cool things with his friends; such as could The Lone Ranger whip Roy Rogers in a fist fight or could Trigger outrun Silver in a race of the two most famous horses in his world? The question of whether or not Aquaman was a true super hero was enough to trigger a fist fight.

Twelve year old boys can trade Superman and Batman comic books for baseball cards of Mickey Mantle and Ken Boyer and later, when they became very valuable, wonder what became of them. He can argue with his brother how in the world the Howard Johnson's Restaurant out on the new highway could possibly have twenty-eight flavors of ice cream as advertised on their huge sign out front. We were only familiar with vanilla and that was after turning a crank for what seemed like four days before the concoction mysteriously became the wonderfully cold and sweet substance we called ice cream. Whoever heard of paying for ice cream? When our dad sped past that particular restaurant in his old Packard it was as if we were driving past the Taj Mahal. Of course, my brother and I would just gape at it because we had no inkling what a Taj Mahal might be. In any case, there was never any danger of us ever setting foot in either place, Howard Johnson's or the Taj Mahal. We were not an "eat out" type family. The first time in my life I ever ate at a sit down restaurant was when I was a teenager and my uncle paid for my meal. Daddy did not believe in what he referred to as "frills" and I believe, now that I am much older, that was his way of saying he could not afford it.

Meanwhile, unbeknownst to the twelve year old, the simple world that had protected him for the first decade of his young life was fast evaporating. His naïve and "wow" world would soon be replaced by confusion and uncertainty; characteristics which would be masked and simmer just beneath the all-knowing surface armor he would soon project to the world as a teenager. It takes a long time to become a real person after enduring several years as a teenager. Parents must develop a thick skin and have the patience of Job until their teenage kids become human once again.

One of the few responsibilities which diverted me away from my care-free twelve year old life style was the odious job of mowing the lawn. To describe the rocky hillside surrounding our house as a lawn was an exaggeration. It was more a hillside beset by rocks and patches of Johnson grass which would have been a challenge to a John Deere with a bush hog. Our machine of choice would have been a nice, self-propelled push mower to navigate the uphill stretches. Instead, our only alternative was an old reel mower which had seen much better days many years before it came to our house to die. Our daddy had a bad habit of rescuing anything he considered useful from alongside the road and I suspect someone else had wisely discarded the machine. A reel mower had no motor and was totally dependent on the human body for an energy source. A well sharpened reel mower would have been the right machine for a flat, manicured green at Augusta National Golf course. It was a lost cause when the mower hit the impenetrable wall of Johnson grass in the lower portion of our yard. It was like Jungle Jim hacking his way through the impassable vines of deep, dark Africa. That green iron curtain of grass called for something even more heinous: a sling blade. This device would have made water- boarding look humane if only our leaders could get one into the hands of those who want to do harm to our country. They would sing like canaries at a bird show after about five minutes in a Johnson grass patch with stalks like field corn. I keep two old sling blades hung on the outside wall of my shop but not for any type of personal usage. They are there strictly for the sake of nostalgia. Anytime I begin to feel sorry for myself because of having to cut grass riding a Cub Cadet with a forty-two inch cut, a twenty horse engine, a padded seat, battery-powered start and even a cup holder, I just remember how it used to be in the good old days with a sling blade and reel mower.

The area directly in front of our house was totally devoid of grass and was swept almost daily with a broom. Sweeping the yard is a practice that has apparently gone out of style and has become a lost art. I am not sure why this was done but that was just the way it was. Everybody swept their front yard. In any event, a patch of gravel free of dirt was put to good use as I learned to field ground balls. Our house was in a very low place

153

and on one side there was a retaining wall between our house and the neighbor on that side. The four foot high wall was ideal to bounce a baseball off of and pretend to play second base for the Yankees. However, this was lethal for our neighbor's potted geraniums she kept atop the wall. It took several years for my young arm to zero in on the wall and many of her plants suffered the consequences until my aim improved. I owe a great debt to Mrs. Jones for her patient and forgiving nature. Her forbearance allowed me to go on to a very mediocre career as a Little Leaguer and high school second baseman.

Another summer event was to build a tree house. Back then kids did the unthinkable and built their own tree house. This is totally unlike today when parents apparently engage an architect and contractor to construct a tree house for their kids which could be lived in year round. Many municipalities even require a building permit for a tree house to be built within their corporate limits. These type restrictions would not have passed muster back in the 1950's. Old barn wood and tin were plentiful in those days and scavenging was a favorite pastime of most boys. As a result, every bunch of boys worth their salt had a proprietary tree house to be used only by permission of the builders. The planning and building created the most excitement because, once completed, it was very boring to simply perch up there for hours at a time. There were no safety codes for tree houses at that time and accidents were not uncommon. As a matter of fact, when I was about six years old I toppled from a tree house built by my older brothers and broke my arm. At the time it wasn't so bad because I was able to miss a whole year of kindergarten. My mother had enrolled me at Maud Lindsay's Free Kindergarten but refused to let me attend with a cast on my arm. She apparently feared I would be unable to protect myself against all the other urchins with only one good arm. There was always the possibility she feared I would use the heavy metal and plaster cast as a weapon and club my classmates senseless. Anyway, this wonderful institution founded by Maud Lindsay was established to help educate the children of mill workers in East Florence when the area was home for many mills and their children were largely uneducated. In the long run I was probably worse off having missed my opportunity to attend this historic school as did all my siblings.

I was very blessed to grow up in very close proximity to a nice little creek which ran through the creek bottom at the foot of the hill on which we lived. It was called Sweetwater Creek and originated at a huge spring on the grounds of an old plantation a couple miles east of our house. The creek served as a playground for all my siblings and other kids in the community and provided more opportunities for play than any Disney park. Of course, fishing and swimming in the creek took up a great portion of our time.

The little creek was also a great place to catch crawfish. After figuring out the little critters could move in only one direction, and that was backward, made them easy prey. Imagination was the only limiting factor when looking for fun things to do around the creek.

My friend Bobby and I came up with one idea that made all the others pale in comparison. It all began when our teacher read the novel, The Kon-Tiki Expedition, to our class at the end of the school year. The author, a Norwegian by the name of Thor Heyerdahl, set out to prove that the Polynesian Islands could possibly have been settled by people from South America. To prove his theory, he constructed a large raft from Balsa wood and attempted to repeat the same journey in 1948. He named the raft Kon-Tiki. Our teacher included this book as an example of a modern day explorer after we had spent the last few weeks of the year studying great explorers of the past like Columbus, Magellan and Hudson. We were so swept up by the idea of exploration that we were actually discussing the topic one day on our way to the creek. This was not a usual topic for us but we were both mesmerized by the idea of a voyage which would keep us out of school for months. We were also fascinated by the name, "Thor." As a matter of fact, I asked my dad if he would call me Thor but he gave me a look which I immediately interpreted to mean, "Don't ever ask me that question again." Most of my friends had never heard of Thor and read nothing heavier than Mad Magazine and idolized Alfred E. Newman, which did not speak well of their intellect or for the future of our country.

Every kid in the holler knew that Sweetwater Creek emptied into the Tennessee River not far from our community. But Bobby and I paid attention in our geography class and we knew that the Tennessee River was a tributary of the Ohio River, which fed into the Mississippi River and that mighty river flowed into the Gulf of Mexico. Once one had reached the waters of the Gulf, the entire world awaited. Our plan was to attempt to float down our creek and reach the river, a distance of not more than two miles. We were not foolish enough to think we could reach the Gulf but we only wanted to test the waters, so to speak, in the event the opportunity for a longer cruise materialized. Just as we began discussing what type of boat we would need for such a journey, by sheer coincidence we happened to be walking past his grandmother's out-building on which hung a huge wash tub. It was large enough for an adult to bathe in and most folks in our neighborhood did exactly that as indoor plumbing was not yet a luxury enjoyed by everyone. We had used this very tub on a number of occasions, without his grandmother's knowledge or permission, when we needed a war drum to announce that Geronimo was going on the war path. When turned upside down it made an ideal war drum. The tub was always returned to the exact nail from which it came with only a few dents in the bottom. His grandmother never noticed the wear and tear because she refused to wear her glasses and as a result was legally blind. We soon found that two twelve year boys barely fit into the large wash tub. It was also a surprise when we further discovered a round wash tub has a tendency to flip over without any warning whatsoever. Consequently, we were only able to travel about two hundred yards downstream, after capsizing numerous times, when we decided to postpone our dream until a more suitable vessel was available. Returning home soaking wet was never a good idea because it made my mother suspicious about what I had been up to. To avoid a nasty reaction for being wet, we killed a couple of hours waiting for our clothes to dry and then began the trek back to his grandmother's house to return the tub to its rightful place on the wall. Unfortunately, we failed to take into account that his grandmother used the tub almost every day or so to wash, soak clothes or bathe and she was frantically searching her yard for the tub. Previously, we had need of the tub only at night and the fact that she might need the tub never crossed our minds.

My previous experience with Bobby's grandmother had been very pleasant and generally involved cookies and milk. She seemed to love her grandson and his friends and, for all practical purposes, was a harmless old lady. On this particular day she was neither pleasant nor harmless and did not mention cookies and milk. Instead, she tore into us with a fury that was quite surprising. As I recall, she made mention of the fact that she did not give a rat's rear end about any man named Thor or any heathens trying to sail across the ocean on a raft. Her main concern seemed to be that her grandson was stupid enough to believe that he could float around in a tub. She used some other words I pretended not to hear because my friend seemed to be embarrassed to hear them come from his grandmother's mouth. Realizing she was not wearing her glasses and her attention was focused entirely on Bobby, it was possible she had not yet recognized me as her grandson's partner in crime. Taking advantage of this fortuitous observation, I chose to slowly slink away and, using her outdoor shed for cover, bolted toward the sanctuary of higher ground. My assessment of the situation was correct and in a short time I was once again enjoying cookies and milk after her grandson had served a probationary period. One of my very first life lessons was that time does heal all wounds.

My last totally free summer with no significant responsibility was in 1963, while I was still in high school. Since that year pretty much all my summers have been consumed by work, school or a combination of the two. Several times during that last, glorious summer some of my buddies and I spent two to three days at a time camped on the river.

In the extreme northwest corner of the state, in an area about thirty miles from our house and encompassing thousands of acres is a game management area known to locals as Panther Creek. It is bordered on the west by the state of Mississippi, on the north by the state of Tennessee and on the south by the Tennessee River. The area is extremely isolated and inhabited by only a few hardy souls, even to this very day. Folks who reside in this area have an aversion to crowds and love to be left alone. Our trips always began by securing the use of a fishing boat from the father of one of our group. Loading the boat with our gear, food, tarps, and assorted other items which we never used, we would set out on our great adventure. There was a very primitive boat ramp at Panther Creek which allowed us to put the boat in the water and park our vehicle until we returned a few days later. After hitting the main river we normally traveled a good distance downstream until we found a wide gravel bar. This became our home for the next several days. Our time was spent fishing out on the river or walking up and down the river bank hoping to catch brim when the willow flies were hatching and then fishing for catfish after dark. Initially, we thought we would sort of live off the land with our fishing but if we hadn't taken Beanie Weenies and bread we would have starved to death. Sensible adults would not normally subject themselves to such conditions but we were having the time of our lives. The boat we were using was about the size of a Boston Whaler and the motor was not much larger than a King Edward cigar box. It was not a very good partnership. Progress up and down the huge river was very slow, even in good conditions. When the wind picked up, it was not only slow but very dangerous.

Late one afternoon, while we were out in the main river channel, we decided to cross over to the Mississippi side and fish a while. Time got away from us and we started back across the river way too late for a safe crossing in the huge boat and small motor. The Tennessee is a very large and beautiful river but it can also be very dangerous. It was so dark one of us had to crouch in the bow with a flashlight hoping to spot floating logs and branches before it was too late. Occasionally a big roller would hit us sideways and water would come into the boat. One of the major failings of a sixteen year old boy is the ability to recognize a dangerous situation. This flaw in their logic is evident by reading the local obituaries. Only after we somehow made it safely back to our camp did I realize the danger we were really in by crossing the middle of the main channel of a huge river at night with no running lights and no life jackets. At times during my life I have reflected back to various predicaments I have been in, mostly as a result of my own stupidity, and that particular night remains close to the top of the list.

Nighttime on the bank of a river like the Tennessee is a cacophony of sound. The waves constantly lap on the beach, the logs on the fire pop, the frogs croak and fish slap the water somewhere out in the dark. Thankfully, we were mostly unaware of the snakes as they slithered around in the dark. Sleeping out in the open with only the sky for a roof under millions of stars made me realize how small and insignificant I really was in the total scheme of things. Watching the moon move across the sky and figuring out the constellations should be on everybody's bucket list. One of the main attractions at night on the river is to watch the long lines of barges make their way ponderously up and down the river. The large searchlight on the bow scanning ahead for sandbars and other boats makes their approach known long before the sound arrives. The broad flat bow of the lead barge creates giant waves which eventually make their way to shore and continue to crash onto the gravel bar long after the line of barges has already passed by. Moments like those give one a lot of time to reflect on what has been and what is to come. Teenage boys have very little to reflect back on, or at least that was my situation, and have no idea what lies ahead.

Knowledge of the future has always seemed to be something everybody claims to want to know about but, in reality, do we really? If, in a flash, we suddenly knew of all the heartaches, sickness, disappointment and death that lie ahead would we be any better off? I think not. The fact that the world seems to be full of palm readers, crystal ball gazers, tea leaf readers and psychics who claim to know it all is ample evidence many folks fear what might lie ahead of them and maybe, if they are warned ahead of time, they will be able to avoid the inevitable. The many times I sat watching the barges churn up and down the river late at night as a teenager did not reveal one single thing about my future. The only certainty that began to form in my mind was that a door was closing in my life and another door was going to open. What might lie behind the new door was an unknown. The days of my boyhood were at an end and a time of responsibility and accountability were beginning to loom on the horizon. As I recall one of my main concerns was how in the world I would survive in this huge world after my parents passed away. Little did I know that my mother would be dead in less than a year and I would soon have my first date with the girl I later married. My mother had a saying that she often used to describe people who were engaged in meaningless activity that, in her estimation, did not amount to anything worthwhile. She would say that person was just "fanning around." The 1950's and early 1960's were a wonderful time to be a boy for me, but my summer time days of "fanning around" were rapidly coming to a close. In a lot of ways, the summer of 1963 was the last real "summertime" of my life. That is not to say there were no more summers; they were just very, very different.

About the Author

Tom McDonald is the youngest of seven children born to William Ervin and Pauline Lindsey McDonald. He spent his boyhood and part of his teenage years living in the East Florence community. Almost his entire family, parents, grandparents, brothers, sister, aunts, uncles and most cousins attended Brandon Elementary School. Mr. McDonald met his future wife, Margo Wilson, while both were students at Central High School. They were married in 1965 and have two children, Amy and Will. Mr. McDonald received his B.S. degree from the University of North Alabama and his M. A. and Ed. S. degrees from the University of Alabama in Tuscaloosa. He retired from the Florence City School system as a counselor at Bradshaw High School. His hobbies include woodworking and day-hiking on the Appalachian Trail. Mr. McDonald resides with his wife near the Cloverdale Community in rural Lauderdale County in Northwest Alabama.

Also by Tom McDonald

When Memories Come Calling, ISBN 978-1-934610-86-2, $14.95

Books by William McDonald

A Walk Through the Past –People and Places of Florence and Lauderdale County Alabama, ISBN 978-0-9719945-6-0, $24.95

Lore of the River – the Shoals Long Ago, ISBN 978-0-9719946-2-1, $18.95

Remembering Sweetwater – the Mansions, the Mills, the People, ISBN 978-0-9719946-3-8, $19.95

Civil War Tales of the Tennessee Valley, ISBN 978-0-9719946-7-6, 17.95

Old North Field, ISBN 978-1-934610-05-3, $14.95

Paths in the Brier Patch, ISBN 978-1-934610-06-0, $14.95

Judi Letters, ISBN 978-1-934610-28-2, $14.95

Bluewater Publications is a multi-faceted publishing company capable of meeting all of your reading and publishing needs. Our two-fold aim is to:

1) Provide the market with educationally enlightening and inspiring research and reading materials.
2) Make the opportunity of being published available to any author and or researcher who desire to be published.

We are passionate about preserving history; whether through the re-publishing of an out-of-print classic, or by publishing the research of historians and genealogists. Bluewater Publications is the *Peoples' Choice Publisher*.

For company information or information about how you can be published through Bluewater Publications, please visit:

www.BluewaterPublications.com

Also check Amazon.com to purchase any of the books that we publish.

Confidently Preserving Our Past,
Bluewater Publications.com

www.ingramcontent.com/pod-product-compliance
Lightning Source LLC
LaVergne TN
LVHW061332060426
835512LV00013B/2611